You Deserve to Love Your Job
How to Find Your Purpose & Enjoy Your Life

By Arlene Pace Green, Ph.D.

Helen,

<u>You</u> deserve it &
the World needs it!

♡, Arlene

You Deserve to Love Your Job

ISBN 978-0-578-77837-2

Published by Conqueror Productions, LLC
Milton, Florida
www.MyConqueror.com

TABLE OF CONTENTS

Introduction

How it All Started

I left my Pastor's office and immediately went home and typed up my resignation letter from my corporate executive role. While it took me 9 months to submit the letter, I made the decision to resign the moment I began typing. Everything I'd experienced in life brought me to that moment. I'd experienced these moments before – the moment you walk out of a door that you know you will never walk into again. I felt it the day I drove out of Virginia to my new home in South Carolina (I had always dreamed of coming back to Virginia with out of state plates). I felt it the moment I walked out of my office in South Carolina 9 months pregnant with my family picture frames in my hand. And I knew it the day I typed my last resignation letter.

The great thing about life is that it's never stagnant. We can always grow, learn, and change; and that is what I hope this book does for you. My hope for you is that this book awakens you to new truths, encourages you to dream again, and enables you to make any transition that is in the direction of your dreams and desires. As an Organizational Psychologist, I have spent my life studying, researching, and thinking about work. I've also had the chance to put that studying, researching, and thinking into practice through 30 years in childcare, consulting, corporate employment, and now business ownership. My goal is to share both the research and my life experiences to help you create a work life that you love. I know that may sound like a dichotomy – work and love; however, you will spend more time at work than in any other single activity in your life. You deserve to love it!

How to Use This Book

Think of this book as a WORK-book. Get ready to think, explore, and take action. *Write in it,* draw pictures ♥, fold pages, underline, or highlight on your electronic device. This book is filled with ideas and action steps that you can take to find your purpose and enjoy your life.

Are you thinking of quitting your job? Awesome – I've quit several. However, this book is not intended to encourage rash decisions until you have fully considered the consequences. Hate your boss or mad at work? Take a vacation – don't quit your job. You can also fast forward to chapter 11 and read it first. Then, come back to the beginning so we can craft a plan to help you love your job and fully enjoy your life.

1

It IS Possible

"It takes courage to grow up and become who you really are."

- E.E. Cummings

It is actually possible to love your job. For real. It is not just for the lucky or special people in this world. It is for you, me, and everyone else who is willing to invest the time and energy needed to construct a work life that you enjoy. For years, I worked a job feeling like there was something else for me – either something was missing that I hadn't found, or something was added that was never supposed to be there in the first place. I was not unhappy per se, but I was unsettled. I wasn't confident that what I was doing was exactly what I was created to do. Fast-forward five years and I am in a very different place. I am doing more of what I love and loving those around me in the process.

The first thing you have to do to find your purpose and create a life you enjoy is to believe that it is possible. It is possible to wake up every morning to a calling, not an alarm clock. It is possible to say "I am having an amazing day" during the middle of the workday and mean it. It is possible to not dread Mondays and not live for Fridays. It is possible to not spend every other day thinking about that one glorious moment when you can retire and finally do what you want to do. It is actually possible to work and live a life that you enjoy; not just on the weekends, but during the week.

If you do not believe it is possible, you will never have it. You will not ask yourself the questions you need to ask. You will not look in the places you need to look. And you certainly will not leave the comfortable place that is meeting your needs, even though it is satisfying very little of your wants.

So, let's start with this. Say this to yourself - "it is possible to love my work." Say it again. How does it feel? Ridiculous? Exciting? Don't question the truth of it yet – just entertain it. If that is something you are willing to entertain, then this book is for you. It is designed to provide you a roadmap of ideas and strategies to get you from where you are today to where you were destined to be. It is based on research, theory, best practice, and the experiences of myself and others who are on this journey. Sound exciting? It is. Sound scary? It is.

Chapter Summary:

- It is possible to love your work and live the life you were created to live.

Take Action:

1. Instead of questioning or challenging the chapter summary, entertain it for the next 7 days. Say it to

yourself over and over, write it on a post-it note and place it where you will see it. For example, write "I will love my work," "I will live the life I was created to live," or "I am on the path to the life I was born to live."

2. Take 15 minutes and write down your thoughts to these questions to get your mind moving in this new direction:

   o What would I do every day if I didn't need money? (Yes, I know we need money, but imagine you don't. Pretend you have hit the lottery. After you take several vacations, rest, and recoup from what you are currently doing, what would you do?)

   o When I was little I wanted to _____ because I like _____.

   o What would I change in the world if I knew it would succeed?

Freebie Alert! You can capture your notes on the book worksheet which can be accessed by visiting www.arlenepacegreen.com/bookresources

2

There is a Process

"Purpose is a thing you build, not a thing you find."

- John Coleman[1]

There is a process you can follow to construct your purpose and build the life you are intended to live. It is interesting how we willingly solve countless problems in our own and others' lives. For example, your best friend is not sure if the person they are dating is right for them? Ask me! Need help with a problem at work? I can help! Interested in debating the political issues of the day? Let's go! But when we are trying to figure out what we should do with our lives...we have no idea....it feels daunting. How is that truly possible? We all have methods we use for solving problems, but for some reason, we rarely apply those same methods to the challenges in our own lives. So not only is there <u>A</u> process, there are a gazillion processes you can use to get to this answer. For the sake of simplicity, I am going to give you a process I have used to get you started.

I like to approach life problems the way I approach business problems. That is through a series of four questions: Why? What? How? And Now? For this chapter, let us start with the first two questions, Why and What.

Starting with Why & What

Why do you work? Yes, you need the money. But beyond that, what is your purpose at work? What do people come to you for the most? Work was created before the fall of Adam and Eve, so it is not just a punishment (really, it's not!). To ensure it does not feel like a punishment, we must uncover the work you were specifically created to do. If you already know the answer to that question, congratulations and skip to chapter 3! If not, let's continue.

Research suggests your purpose is most often found through your own intentional efforts. People that spend time in career exploration, planning, and thinking, are more likely to discover it. Those individuals also report higher levels of career and life satisfaction.[2] Can you stumble across your purpose early in life or in a moment in time? Absolutely. Diego Rivera began drawing at a young age after the loss of his twin brother. Katherine Johnson solved complex math problems early in life; finishing eighth grade at 10 years old and graduating with a Mathematics and French degree by 18. However, research suggests that this instant or early understanding of our purpose is rare. For most of us, purpose is something that is created and built over time. It is discovered through practice, trial, error, and the evolution of our thinking. That is certainly the experience that I have had, and it started with my college major.

I was living in Virginia and attending James Madison University. Based on my life experiences at the ripe age of 18, I had narrowed my career choices down to being an elementary school teacher or a psychologist. I took a class in education and thought, not bad, this could be it. That summer, I worked as a YMCA Day Camp Counselor for 7 and 8 year olds. While I loved the job, I quickly learned that I barely had the demeanor to get the kids to learn a game, never mind learn to read. I was overly nice and lots of fun, but did not have the disciplinary mindset or desire to keep order in a classroom (even later as a parent, one of my friends called me 'cream puff'). So I abandoned education and began pursuing psychology, but there were so many fields of psychology to choose from. I thought I wanted to be a psychiatrist, but when I volunteered in a mental health facility I realized that wasn't for me. Next, I considered becoming a family counselor. I took a group counseling class where I found myself distracted while others talked about their problems and seriously hated sharing my own stories - I dreaded going to that class. Finally, I took an organizational psychology class. It focused on a business environment which was faster paced, future focused, and better aligned with how I like to work. After that I still had to figure out if I wanted to go to graduate school, try to get a job in consulting, or teach. Like it did for me, discovering your purpose will likely take work and time. It may not appear in a dream like Salvador Dali's paintings or Albert Einstein's theory of relativity. You are most likely to uncover your purpose while actively exploring, asking questions, and working to understand the different options that are available.[2,3] The exploration is actually part of the fun.

One way to explore the question of purpose is by asking those who know you best – yourself and those around you.[4] To begin this step, let's conduct an experiment. The experiment's steps are at the end of this chapter. As you gather the data from your experiment, I want to provide some context that may help you put the data you gather to use.

Pursue Clarity Though It May Look Different Than You Think

Spend the time needed to give yourself the gift of clarity. If it does not come today, don't worry or beat yourself up! I have a journal that I use to write my dreams and ideas as they come to me. Sometimes my answers are immediate and sometimes they are cultivated over weeks and years. But with consistent focus, they always come. Be patient with yourself and enjoy the process. There are so many stories of people finding their enduring purpose at various ages of life. Jack Ma founded Alibaba at 35, Mary Kay Ash started Mary Kay Cosmetics at 45, Julia Childs published her first cookbook at 49, and Winston Churchill became England's Prime Minister at 62. This is not to say that the things they were doing before weren't purposeful, as they may have been. However, for many of us it all comes together later in life than we might hope or expect.

It is possible that your purpose will not look the way you are envisioning it.

I am so tired of hearing people say "follow your passion!" You too? "Following your passion" is a concept that emerged in the 1990s and has become popularized over time[5]. It creates a belief that our purpose in life is tied to one job or focus area that once found, will dominate the rest of our lives. We believe that we will discover that we are supposed to be a writer, a painter, a surgeon, or a business owner. Once we know it, we will pursue that single career our entire lives, and that alone will give our life purpose. Is that possible? Sure. But let me give you some ideas and research on other ways your purpose can develop.

Different Purposes for Different Times

Clarity is an evolving concept. As one question is answered, another one appears. As you explore certain options, other options are created. There are certainly some people who discover and pursue a single focus for the rest of their lives. In his Stanford commencement speech, Steve Jobs famously described being inspired and driven by the dream of Apple since he was 20. However for most of us, purpose(s) will emerge and evolve over time. Sometimes it starts with knowing what you don't want to be. Oprah Winfrey reported watching her Grandmother boil and hang clothes on a line for a living and thinking to herself "that won't be me." Some of us will engage in multiple and different purposes across different periods of our lives. I moved from a corporate job to business ownership to writing. I loved each of those phases, and all of them taught me things that helped me in the next phase of life. Remain open to the fact that as you change and evolve over time, so may your purpose.

Purpose in <u>How</u> You Live

Your purpose may be more focused on *how* you live than *what* you do. I created my first mission statement during a week-long program at a 4H campsite. We completed a life-map activity and from that came my first mission – "to live life on purpose." I even had a graphic (see below). For me, this graphic meant that I was in the places I found myself for a reason; and because of that, I wanted to act on the purpose for which I was there. That mission impacted me in large and small ways. In meetings, if I felt I should say this or that, I would say it. If I felt I should participate in this organization or that activity, I would do it. It gave me a sense of courage and direction for the choices I made on a daily basis. It did not illuminate *what* I should be doing, but it definitely governed how I showed up.

My current purpose statement is to inspire and help others identify and attain their greatest aspirations. I certainly get to do that in my business as a coach and organization consultant. I also get to do that in conversations with my friends, in the faith-based leadership podcast I share with two friends (Kingdom Leadership on Apple Podcast – check it out!), and with my daughter and her friends when we spend time together. I also pray I am doing that with this book! Your purpose may be a particular job, but it may also be a way of interacting, a way of giving, or a way of being that can show up across many different jobs. I do not have to work a certain job to help people achieve their greatest aspirations and dreams. Your purpose may be beyond or outside of a job as well.

Pursue Purpose & Happiness

My first mission statement, to live life on purpose, was also a rejection of a life built on happiness alone. At the time, when asked about the purpose of life, many people would say 'to be happy.' I always felt that was a bit naïve, and perhaps even shallow. The things that make me happy are not a replica of the things that give my life joy and meaning. If I wanted to be happy,

15

I would never clean the kitchen and spend a couple hours a day riding my bike and bird watching. So instead of focusing on what makes me happy only (cake anyone?!), my purpose is tied to what brings meaning, joy, and impact. In what spaces am I uniquely created to make things better and add value? By the way, those things also make me happy most of the time, but happiness is not my ultimate goal.

Living on purpose has placed me in difficult and challenging places where I was anything but happy. I have had to tell people their jobs were going away, I have been put on a performance improvement plan and nearly fired, and I have stayed up countless nights wondering if I made the right decisions with my career and relationships. I wouldn't change one minute of it. Every experience pushed me further into maturity and closer to my purpose. I challenge you to pursue a life of purpose and meaning, not only happiness. Happiness comes and goes. Purpose is a constant.

Let's Begin

So let me ask you again: what are you created to do and why? Draw a picture, create a statement, or write down your thoughts. For the last 20 years, my mission statements have given me a foundation on which to build a life and make life decisions. A level of clarity on your purpose is a gift. It provides a compass for your decisions and a path for action. Without clarity, it is difficult to find the motivation or make the right choice when opportunities arise. The clearer the path, the more likely you are to act and attain what you envision.[6,7]

Chapter Summary:

- Discovering your purpose may take time, exploration, trial and error.
- How do you currently solve the problems of your life? How can you apply that same approach to uncovering your purpose?
- Your purpose may look different over time.
- Your purpose may not be a job.
- Your purpose may be tied to how you live.
- Pursue a life of purpose and meaning, and happiness will come.

Take Action:

1. Complete the experiment that follows.
2. Spend time in silence. People can inspire your purpose, but it must be birthed and decided from the inside out. Spend time with YOU. Alone. In silence.
3. Honor your dreams and outlandish ideas. I am not saying change jobs today based on a dream (though I am not against it either – see chapter 11), but I am encouraging you to write all of your ideas down and explore them fully. Honor them as real possibilities.

4. Draft a purpose statement. Most purpose statements identify what you want to do, how you want to do it, and or who you want to serve. A sample purpose statement is "I will serve _____ (who?) by ___ (doing what?) using _____ (with what skills?)."

Freebie Alert! *You can capture your draft purpose statement on the book worksheet which can be accessed by visiting www.arlenepacegreen.com/bookresources .*

Conduct Your Purpose Experiment

1. Identify seven amazing people that you trust and who know you well. Don't wimp out at four or five; find seven. They can be friends, co-workers, peers, family, anyone you trust has your best interest at heart. Ideally, choose people from a few different settings; meaning, a few family members, a few friends, a few co-workers, etc.

2. Send each of them the email below. Feel free to customize it of course! Once you type the email, you may think, "I shouldn't send this! I don't want to put myself out there like that. It looks like I'm begging for compliments!" Turn OFF those voices in your head and send it anyway.

3. Send each person a follow-up text to ensure they actually

read and respond to the email.

4. Once at least three of the seven have responded, print out their responses. Don't skip this step. I know the tendency is to read everything electronically, but that won't work for this. There is power in the written word, so print out their responses.

5. Block a 1-Hour period where you are by yourself with no distractions.

6. Read each person's response. Underline the key words or phrases.

7. Go back and read the underlined phrases and write down any themes or patterns – meaning things that are said by more than one person.

8. Review the list of themes and place a star next to those that give you energy, excite you, and are things you would love to do…every day.

9. Are there discrepancies? Things people say that are different than what you expected? Ask yourself why. Write the discrepancies down so you can think about them over time.

10. Are there things that cause you to think "I could never do that!?" Resist the temptation to evaluate the feasibility of each idea. Instead, just write it down and ask yourself if it sounds like something you'd like to do…. every day.

11. Go back to the action steps and turn your insights into a purpose statement.

Sample Email:

Hi Shawn!

I'm doing an experiment and need your help. Can you answer each of the 3 questions below and get it back to me by Friday, August 23? I would GREATLY appreciate your thoughts, ideas, and creativity. I'm using your responses, and the responses of others, as wise counsel in helping me figure out some next steps.

1. *When have you seen me at my best?*
2. *If you had to hire me to do one thing for you, what would that be?*
3. *If I told you I was starting a new business, what type of business would you guess that it would be?*

Thank you and love you much!!
Arlene

3

Build Whole-Life Dreams

"Your work is very personal."

– Arlene Pace Green

The western concept of work-life balance is flawed. The image often shared is your work on one side of the scale, your personal life on the other, and you (and me!) in the middle trying miserably to balance the two (see graphic). In my experience, this is a false dichotomy and analogy. Why? Because work is very personal. And having an amazing personal life WILL take work. The friendships you make through work, the partnerships you establish, the skills you gain, the work you accomplish – all of those are very personal, and all of those things can and will impact the other areas of your life. As a result, I no longer have a Work plan and a Personal plan – I have a Life Plan which integrates the two.

Research now suggests that an integrated model is more reflective of our lives and wellbeing.

Research has found that those who like their jobs are twice as likely to be happy with their overall lives. They are also sick less often, feel like time moves faster during the day, and are more engaged in other aspects of their life.[1]

When I separated my work and personal life into different buckets, it also gave me permission to hold myself to different standards in each setting. My work life may be killing me, but I sure do love my family! My family life is a mess, but I am doing great at work! Huh? That way of thinking gives us a false perception of *balance*. Embedded in the concept is that you cannot have it all, or at least that you cannot have it all at the same time. Do we really believe two different realities can peacefully co-exist in one person? Can you genuinely be happy for 12 hours a day if you are miserable for the other 12? That's not to say that we cannot achieve different levels of success in different areas of our lives. It's certainly possible to kill it at work and suck at home. I know; I've done it. And those two groups of people may have totally different opinions of you. However, it is not possible that one area does not *affect* the other, because at the end of the day, they both affect YOU. I'll tell you my story.

For twenty years, I worked in various corporate roles. With each role, I took on more accountability, responsibility, and complexity. I loved it. I was well thought of at work and truly believed I could take my career in any direction I wanted. At home, I was doing so-so at best. I am married to an amazing husband and partner who could not be any easier to live with and was always incredibly supportive. I have one daughter and she is remarkably kind, intelligent, and thoughtful. So, while they were not telling me there were problems at home, there were definitely problems at home. With more responsibility at work, I became increasingly less present at home. The worst part was that I did not even realize it. I did not realize that I was paying less attention to my family. I did not realize that my friendships were becoming more shallow. I did not realize that I was living a largely selfish life, driven by my need to succeed at work. Thankfully I reached a place in my career where I was no longer satisfied with work. I wanted something different and decided to "try this entrepreneurship thing for a while."

Within two weeks of stepping away from my previous role, my whole life changed, and I am not exaggerating. I started noticing my daughter like I hadn't in years. I noticed her strengths and the challenges she was facing in a way I never had. I felt like I could breathe, rest, and spend more time with God. Almost immediately, God brought me different work opportunities. I took them on with joy, but the context was so different, that they did not come with the stress or non-stop need to be present that I had previously. I was in the "start-up high" of just opening a business. Everything is rosy, the opportunities are endless, and the workload is low. It wasn't long before the workload started to increase, but once I experienced a new normal of rest and peace, there was no way I was going back to my previous state of mind. Instead, I grew the business in a largely balanced way - hiring others to take on key responsibilities and allowing me to keep what I had gained - the gift of being present with my faith, my family, my clients, my friends, and myself. I still have very long nights and weeks of intense work. There are also stretches of days or weeks where my connection with my family or friends is lessened. Both of those are a part of my new reality. However, I *can* say that I don't feel guilty for either. I love that my daughter watches me and her Dad work hard in fulfilling the commitments we have at work – that's life. I just appreciate that those commitments are not so completely overwhelming that I am losing touch with all of the other areas of my life for long stretches at a time.

Now while this has been my journey, it is certainly not the right journey for everyone. You may want your life to be largely focused on your work endeavors, with just a few intimate personal relationships. Or you may want to be a stay-at-home parent, with your work focused on managing your household or family life. Or perhaps you are called to travel the world as a geographic photographer making friends and creating relationships along the way (that honestly sounds amazing if my family would come along). What you decide is up to you, as long as you are doing it with a clear understanding of the impact of your choices on EVERYTHING that matters to YOU.

I also recognize that our finances can impact this area greatly. When I was in my early 20s, I was in graduate school and receiving a $10K a year stipend for living expenses. My parents had given me a car and were thankfully still paying the insurance, but I was covering everything else. To make ends meet, I worked several odd jobs during that time – waitressing in a hotel dining room, temporary office work, and various projects with my school. Even though I needed the money, I quit several of those jobs for work-life balance reasons. The waitressing job started at 5:00 in the morning and I had classes that ended at 9:00 at night, not including studying. I remember thinking late one night, "I just can't do it anymore." I decided to spend less on groceries instead (who needs meat?!) and went to the hotel dining room that night and dropped off my apron and a hand-written resignation. Balance at that time of my life meant avoiding exhaustion if at all possible.

As I look back, I do not regret quitting the waitressing job and cutting back on groceries. I also do not regret the twenty years I spent in corporate roles. In fact, I loved and grew from both of those experiences. I am simply grateful that I have since moved into a different way of living. A way in which what I do for work *adds* to my personal life versus taking away from it. My work and personal life are no longer in competition – in fact, they are merged into one beautiful life. I certainly focus on one area at a time for much of my day, but I have lost the guilt that comes from believing that investing in one area is somehow detracting from the other. I have also dropped the faulty belief that one area is somehow compartmentalized from the others. I have received work emails that throw me off and negatively affect my thoughts for days at a time. Similarly, my last venture to the State Fair (everything is bigger in Texas!) gave me a joyful lift for days. I now understand that the different roles in my life are additive – not separate, and not in competition.[2]

I am not a math genius, but I live with two of them. For my Math and Engineering friends, I would say it like this:

Arlene's Previous & Incorrect Perspective on Life:

Personal Life Investments ≥ Work Life

Investments = Beautiful Life

Arlene's Current Perspective on Life:

Personal Life Investments x Work Life

Investments = Life Satisfaction

Now it is time to go back to your purpose statement or drawing and add the other elements of your life you may not have included. If you only focused on work, focus on the other aspects of your life that are important to you. An approach to try is below.

Think about the most important aspects of your life. I used Faith, Family, Enelra (my business), Fun, Health, and Community. Others to consider might be Relationships, Finance, Career, Romance, Personal Growth or Travel. It does not matter how many areas you choose since there is no one right answer. Creating a life you desire is more like ice skating than speed skating. There is not a single finish line. Some of us may lean in on speed and grace, others may lean in on artistry and acrobatics. There isn't a single answer for everyone, but there is a right answer for you.

Your goal is to create a Whole Life Plan with your purpose at the center. I have one that I review a few times a year. I always consider it a work in progress because who knows when I am going to learn, grow, and change. Looking at it helps me reflect on the extent to which my life is in alignment with my purpose. It is both motivating and affirming at the same time, and I want the same for you.

Chapter Summary:

- Your work is very personal.
- It will take work to have the life you desire.
- Your experience in one area of your life (e.g., work) will absolutely affect the other areas of your life (e.g., family).

- Create and live whole-life dreams. Think about all the aspects of your life that are important to you and ensure your purpose is well integrated across the various aspects of your life.

Take Action:

1. With your purpose statement at the center, add other areas related to your whole life. Consider areas where you would like to focus for the next few years. Some categories to consider are Faith, Career, Family, Fun, Relationships, Community, Personal Growth, Romance, or anything else that is important to you.
2. Consider how your purpose can be fulfilled in those other areas.
3. Edit and build on your purpose statement and Whole Life Plan based on new insights or ideas.

Freebie Alert! Need Life Plan ideas? You can view a snippet of my life plan by visiting www.arlenepacegreen.com/bookresouces

4

Know Your Starting Point

"Until you make the unconscious conscious, it will
direct your life and you will call it fate."

- C.G. Jung

If you completed the experiment in Chapter 2 and the follow-up
activity in Chapter 3, you should now have an idea of something
you might like to do, become, have, or explore. Not necessarily a
final answer, but at least a fuzzy description of something you
would like to explore in the future. Perhaps your purpose is tied
to starting an online business, changing careers, or moving to a
different position in your current organization. Whatever it is, it
is time to dig deeper into this idea. The path to your purpose can
be illuminated by conducting a deep-dive gap analysis. Where are
you today? Where do you want to be? How do you propose
getting there?

To do this, we are going to use the Work Evaluation model.
Versions of this model have been used by thousands to evaluate
their current work, work they are considering, and in what
direction they would like to take their work going forward. I have
edited the model so you can use it to evaluate any work of
interest. I use the term *work* loosely to mean any endeavor in
which you are investing your time, energy, and resources. This

does not have to mean the activity that pays you money. For example, I recently signed up to volunteer with a local shelter. They do not pay me for the work, but I could certainly use this model to evaluate this work. Let us explore how the model works.

First, identify a body of work that you want to evaluate. It could be your current job, the job you want, your side-hustle, your volunteer activity, or any other area in which you are currently invested or are considering investing in the future. To complete the evaluation, there are three questions to ask and answer for yourself.

ONE: Is the work an area of strength? Is it an area where you are gifted and have invested the time and energy needed to turn this gift into a strength? Being gifted or naturally talented does not automatically make something a strength. I may have the nimble fingers of a pianist, but unless I have spent hours in front of the keys, it is unlikely that playing the piano is a strength. Similarly, I could have a natural ability with numbers, but that does not mean I am a gifted accountant. Operating at a high level at anything requires us to invest in the natural talents we have been given. Imagine a student who is naturally gifted at long-distance running but does not practice before running her first marathon. How likely is it that she will perform well in that race? On the other side, let us not be modest either! If you're killing it, say so! If it is a strength, you probably have evidence of such --

30

for example, feedback from others, comments from the purpose experiment in chapter one, the way you feel when performing the task, or the impact the work is having on others. So the first question is, "is this body of work a strength?" Yes or No. I know there are shades of gray, but for the purposes of this exercise, choose Yes or No.

TWO: Is the work something that does or will likely bring you joy? Meaning, do you enjoy or believe you would enjoy doing it? Does the work give you energy? Is it something that excites you? If someone told you that at some time in the future (but they cannot tell you when), you would be able to do *just this work*, how does that make you feel? If that excites you, it is probably something that brings you joy. When you are doing work you love, it does not matter when the work comes to its ultimate fruition, as long as you get to keep doing it. If that question is demotivating, and the time it takes to fully invest in the work is a factor, your work may not be bringing you as much joy as it could. So, the second question is 'does this body of work bring you joy most of the time?' Again, choose Yes or No.

THREE: Is the work valued in the world _and_ do you want to offer it to others? By *valued*, you are asking if someone would pay you to do it. Generally, people will pay for work they value. However, we know that the world is fickle and times change. What is not valued today may be highly valued tomorrow. There are so many amazing artists whose work wasn't appreciated during their lifetime. Van Gogh sold one painting during his lifetime, reportedly for $109 dollars. So this is not to say that if the work is not valued, you should stop doing it. However, knowing where the work is today will help you uncover your next steps. So, without feeling judged one way or the other, ask yourself if the work is currently valued in the world *today* and if you would want to offer it to others? Are other people being paid or asked to do the type of work you are doing or considering? And if so, would you like to be paid for doing it as well?

Currently, the most sought after-jobs in the United States are in technology and health care.[1] The most prominent non-profits are in human rights, arts, and child advocacy.[2] People are seeking talented people to do all kinds of work from organizing their closets to building their homes. My daughter recently introduced me to 'finger tutting'. If you are not aware, it is when someone moves their fingers in rapid rhythms for others to watch, often in sync with music. I initially would have said there are very few people looking for someone to do 'finger tutting'; but then I searched it on YouTube. There are finger tutting videos with over 14 million views. So even for something as obscure as finger tutting, someone is looking for it. The question for you is, are there people looking for the kind of work you are doing or want to do, and would you like to offer it to them?

If people are looking for it, but you do not want to offer it to them, your answer is No. In reality, there are times we want to do things just for ourselves and that is okay; in fact, it can be rejuvenating. I recently began sewing. I enjoy watching the rhythm of the sewing machine as it makes each stitch. I like to sew slowly – I find it relaxing. While other people may be looking for experts in sewing (of which I am not), I would never want to offer it to the world or get paid to do it. I might offer it to my family, but at this point, that is about it.

Now that you have your answer to the three questions, it is time to plot them on the table. A chart follows that can also help you in making the assessment.

Is the work a Strength?	Is the work a source of Joy (do I like it)?	Is this work relevant to others *and* would you like to offer it to them? (If you answer No to either question, your answer is NO)	What Your Answer Reveal About Your Work
YES	YES	YES	You've Found a Career.
YES	YES	NO	You've Found a Hobby.
NO	YES	YES	You've Found a Dream.
YES	NO	YES	You've Found a Job
YES	NO	NO	You've Found Potential.
NO	YES	NO	You've Found an Interest.
NO	NO	YES	You've Found a Dead End.
NO	NO	NO	

Before we dive into each specific result, let's start with how you can use this information. Regardless of where you are, that does not have to be where you end up. For example, you may have a dream today that you want to turn into a career tomorrow. Or you may have an interest that you would like to make a hobby by investing in it more fully. Without judgment, examine where this body of work is for you today. Then consider where you would like it to be in the future.

Based on your evaluation, what do you have? Read on to learn more about that area.

A Career:

Congratulations! Some people go their entire lives without realizing what it is to have a labor of love--work that you enjoy, that you have invested in to become a strength, and other people value you doing it. If this is not what you are currently getting paid to do, use the rest of this book to create a plan to get there. Joy awaits!

A Hobby:

What many of us need, you have found – a hobby! Hobbies add so many benefits to our lives. First, having a hobby is known to decrease stress and increase physical health, even for hobbies that do not require a great deal of activity like knitting.[3] People with hobbies also tend to be more satisfied with their work and have a lower likelihood of burn-out.[4,5] Joy in any area of your life is a boost to all areas of your life. My husband is an outdoor enthusiast – it is his happy place. If you have found one of your happy places, congratulations! Continue to invest your time in keeping it that way.

A Dream:

Ahhhh….dreams. It is amazing how motivational and instructive a dream can be. Dreams provide clarity and ideas for our future.[6] At one point, this book was a dream. I had an interest in doing it and I believed others would find it valuable, but I had no idea where to start. Enter my first book publisher's conference. And afterwards, the numerous articles, podcasts, posts, conversations, and financial investments that followed. If you are interested in turning your dream into some or all of your career's work, it is time to invest in turning this area into a strength. What classes can you take? How can you gain additional experience? Who can you talk to who holds the knowledge and can teach you about your next steps? If you are interested in turning your dream into a career, use the rest of this book to create a plan to get there. Your calling awaits!

A Job:

You have found a job! And by the way, we all have jobs. Meaning, we all have work that we do that others need from us, that we likely have some strength in, but we honestly do not enjoy. I know filmmakers who hate editing; business owners who hate selling; and how many of us enjoy answering email? Not many according to research, even though office-workers spend between 20-50% of their time doing just that. The question is not *if* you have a job, but rather, what percentage of the work you do *feels* like a job, and whether you're comfortable with that percentage. If you are happy with it, great! If you want to spend less time on work that you do not enjoy, it is time to identify other work that would bring you a greater sense of joy (see Chapter 2). Once you have a sense of what that work might be, you can use the rest of this book to create a plan to get you there.

Potential:

Potential is defined as something that exists in possibility; it is something capable of developing into actuality.[7] When you have a strength in a certain area, this area has the potential of turning into something more -- if you want it to. The question to ask is if this is something you are interested in pursuing further. I personally vote yes on your behalf, and let me tell you why. If you are gifted in an area, there is probably a reason for it, and you may not know that reason until you've fully explored it. I learned in high school that I am gifted in speech-writing. I was preparing to give remarks at a luncheon, and I can still remember the last line of the speech that I delivered to city officials and school administrators: "so please keep us in your thoughts, as we keep you in our prayers." Boom! Cue the standing ovation and applause! Hey, that was pretty good for a high schooler. However, that did not mean I enjoyed giving speeches. I still don't. I enjoy having conversations. Depending upon the environment of the speaking engagement, I either love it or hate it. I never would have known that if I had not continued to engage in various speaking opportunities. The same may be true for you. Just because you have a strength, and you have only used it one way, does not mean that same strength couldn't be used in an entirely different environment and bring you joy at the same time. If you have a strength in a certain area, I encourage you to fully explore it. Learn enough about it, do enough with it until you have a firm answer as to whether or not it is a part of your calling. If you are good at it, my sneaking suspicion is that you are going to need it and want it at some point in your life.

An Interest:

Excellent, you have found an area to explore! An interest is a signal to follow your curiosity. Who knows where it will take you? It may take you to a hobby, a career, a job, or a dead end. But you will not know until you explore it. What are things you can do to learn more about this area? How can you spend time with others who do this well? How can you experience this area for yourself? Whatever those things are, do them and continue doing them until you feel certain if this is something you should pursue or abandon. Either answer is acceptable!

A Dead End:

If it is not a strength and it does not spark joy, it is time to move on from this work. In today's world, it is hard to survive doing work that you do not perform very well. If you are not interested in it, it will be hard to find the motivation to build the skillset necessary for success. Create an exit plan to move on from this work.

Chapter Summary:

- Once you know your purpose and what you would like to do, the next step is to use the Work Evaluation model to evaluate how this work fits or could fit into your life today.
- Knowing where you are today illuminates the path for how you will get from where you are to where you want to be.

Take Action:

1. Use the Work Evaluation Model to evaluate the body of work you are considering.
2. Read the paragraph associated with your answer.
3. Write down insights you gained from this model and any potential actions steps you are now considering.

Part 1 Summary

Look In: Building Your Purpose

Well done! You have completed Part 1. At this time, you should have a fuzzy to somewhat focused idea of what you want to do and why. If not, no problem! Keep reading and exploring. As ideas come to you, capture them on the book worksheet.

"What's the world for you if you can't make it up the way you want it?"

- Toni Morrison

"I am my own muse. I am the subject I know best. The subject I want to better."

- Frida Kahlo

5

Power is Not a Dirty Word

"There are a lot of incentives to stay where you are…even when you hate it."
– Arlene Pace Green

Power is not a dirty word. I have taught a few classes on Power and Influence, and in every class, there are people who have a visceral and negative reaction to the word "power." Unfortunately, many of us have been subjected to people who abuse the power they have. Racism, sexism, physical abuse, ineffective parenting, bullying, mean-spirited colleagues, poor leadership, biased teachers, and the list goes on. We have had so many bad experiences with people in power, that we think power itself is a bad concept and something to be avoided. Nothing could be further from the truth.

Power is neutral. It is a force. That force can be used for good just as well as evil. Dr. Martin Luther King, Jr. had power. Mahatma Gandhi had power. Ida B. Wells had power. The best manager or leader you ever worked for had power. One of my favorite managers and dearest friends used to say, "It's good to be Queen," and I agree. It is great to be in charge. When you are in charge, you have the opportunity to do a great deal of good for your team and those around you. But unfortunately, our negative experiences with power can lead us to avoid assuming or using our power altogether.

Power is simply the capacity to influence. You have power when you have the ability to *"affect others' beliefs, attitudes, and courses of action."*[1] When applied to ourselves, we can say that we have power when we demonstrate the ability to change our own beliefs, attitudes, and actions. So, the first person you must to be able to influence is yourself – and often, we can be our greatest challenge. I can hear you saying, "Not me! I'm in complete control of my life!" Statistics suggest otherwise my friend. Relinquishing our power happens in subtle and insidious ways.

A recent study revealed that 34% of employees are engaged at work. That is, 34% of us are "involved in, enthusiastic about and committed to [our] work."[2] That means that the majority of us, are *not* those things, and 16% of us actually hate where we work. Another 65% of us would rather fire our boss than receive a pay raise.[3] We spend more time at work than in any other activity in our life. So if we are unhappy doing what we do *most often*, and are not actively doing something to change the situation, or at least to change our attitude about the situation, we have to ask ourselves why. Research suggests numerous reasons why we don't change negative situations in our lives. While there is less conclusive evidence on why people stay in bad jobs, there is a lot of research on why people stay in bad relationships. I am not talking about abusive relationships. I am talking about dissatisfying, not fun, bad relationships. Most of it relates to our abhorrence of change. To resist change, we will do just about anything to stay where we are; including denying or avoiding the power that we have. Let's replace "relationship" with "job" and see what we can learn from the research on staying in unhappy places. Take the assessment below by putting a checkmark by anything that sounds familiar. Once complete, read the descriptions that follow to learn more about your checks.

Top 13 Reasons We Stay in Bad ~~Relationships~~ Jobs

1. **Low expectations.** We expect work to suck. When it does, our low expectations are met! To support this, we surround ourselves with friends who hate their jobs too so we have someone fun to complain with.[4,5,6] This belief is reinforced when we think there are only low-quality alternatives available, including not working at all. This solidifies our belief that changing would only produce the same result, and 'ain't nobody got time for that.'

2. **We focus on the positives.** "Yes, I hate what I do every day, but I have great benefits!" We have an amazing ability to focus on the positives with a myopic and unrealistic view of what else is going on. Over time, we tell ourselves that the positives being offered are the ones we care about the most, giving us a reason to stay where we are.

3. **I need the money.** Yes, you need the money; we all need the money. But needing the money is not the same as not being able to leave. Money comes to you. If this is your only reason for staying, think long and hard about it before settling on this option.[7]

4. **We enjoy fantasizing about something else.** It's the fairy tale. When we were younger, some of us imagined that we would do different work than what we are currently doing. That fantasy can seem much greener and happier than the work we are doing today. Many times, we torture ourselves with the idea of what could have been, without actually knowing if that would have made us happier or not. "I could have been a professor with summers off!" That was my favorite form of self-torture every summer while I was working. While it may be hard to explore fantasy relationships (and perhaps you should not), it is not hard to explore fantasy jobs. But instead of exploring it and learning if that is something we actually want to do, we just fantasize about it and keep ourselves in a form of work purgatory – always wishing for something we will never work to have.

5. **I can't do anything about it anyway.** We have learned to be helpless. I don't know how to find a job. I can't use technology. I can't move. We can identify lots of reasons why we can't do anything about our situation. In reality, we can, even if we choose not to. Take the first step and stop saying can't. While in some circumstances, that may be true – it is rare. Typically, the more accurate perception is that we are

choosing not to or just do not want to. There is nothing wrong with staying where you are, but let's be honest about the choices we are making and why.

6. **Squirrel!** As one writer said, staying in a bad ~~relationship~~ job is a "massive distraction".[8] As long as I am thinking and talking about what is wrong with my job or manager, I do not have to think about what is wrong with me. Perhaps my skills are outdated, I need to go back to school, I need to work on my attitude, my relationships stink, or I could work harder. Whatever IT is, complaining about my job keeps me from doing anything about me.

7. **Good old-fashioned self-sabotage.** Sometimes we create an over-arching excuse that is our "go-to" for not doing anything that appears scary or uncertain. Research suggests it can be physical (sore arm, easily winded, tired, a chronic condition) or psychological (interview anxiety, phobias, shyness). While each of these conditions could absolutely impact our ability to change, we humans also have the tendency to give them more power than we ought, and to use them as a crutch for not doing what we could. Do you have a built-in reason for not doing what you know you should or could?[9]

8. **They should do better.** I am an optimist and a realist. I like positive things and positive people – cue the rainbows and unicorns please! However, let me tell you an inconvenient truth – people change because they want to, not because you want them to, and not because you believe they should. Often times, we spend energy thinking and complaining about the

way things should be, even though the people who need to change have no interest in doing so. If you have credible evidence or enduring faith that things are going to change, awesome! Lean in and be the change you want to see. If you have credible evidence that the people in charge are not interested in changing, make your plans accordingly. This is a sneaky way we give away our power. We focus on changes someone else should make instead of the changes we have the power to make for ourselves. You may be 100% completely and totally right about the changes someone else should make. As humans, I am sure there are changes that all of us should be making. And perhaps you staying in your current environment is a light to others and will eventually turn the tide. That may be your calling. If so, great! Just be certain it's not a rationale for staying where you are and avoiding the hard work of making changes in your life where you can.

9. **I am too invested.** I once met a medical doctor who said she hated her job. To become a doctor, you have invested somewhere in the range of two hundred thousand dollars and 11 years of study. Can you imagine getting to the end of that process and realizing you hate your job? Ouch. While it would be a hard pill to swallow, I think it is harder to imagine investing the rest of the one life you have pursuing something you hate. We often focus on what we will lose instead of what we will gain; and that evaluation keeps us where we are.

10. **Meh.** We love it and we hate it. Positive and negative feelings can co-exist. There may be things we love about a

job and also things we hate. When those are in balance, there may not be enough motivation to leave. When your feelings about a job are "meh", getting the energy needed to create a resume, update social media, connect with your network, etcetera, may sound like more work than you are interested in doing.

11. **Timing.** We are prioritizing other areas of our life so the level of enjoyment we have at work is not a priority right now. Given how much time we spend at work, it has to be something really big going on elsewhere. Perhaps we are new parents, newly married, or deeply involved in a hobby or side-hustle that takes all of our extra attention.[10] If now is not the time, no problem! You can create your plan and decide to execute it when you are ready.

12. **We like the status.** Our occupation is a critical component of our social status.[11] Even if we hate what we are doing, the status and recognition we receive from working at a certain place can make it hard to leave. To leave, your status and self-worth must be built on things outside of the organization. I learned the occupational status hierarchy pretty quickly when I started my own business. When you work for a large company, other people are impressed. When you say you work for yourself or a company people have never heard of, they are significantly less impressed.

13. **Suffering is good for me.** Many of us believe that staying in difficult places builds character and makes us better. There is certainly research to support the idea that growth can occur

during challenging times. However, challenging is different from dissatisfying. If you are valuing the learning on a spiritual journey, you are likely making the environment better and not complaining about being there every single day. So, "to thine own self be true."

Now that you have read the list and placed a check by the numbers that sound accurate for you, consider what they indicate about your *power* and *motivation*. First, circle the numbers that you checked in the model that follows. Next, total up the number of checks in each box. Where do you have the most checks? Are you balanced across a few of the boxes? Read on to learn more about your results and what you can do if you would like to change them.

POWER X MOTIVATION MODEL

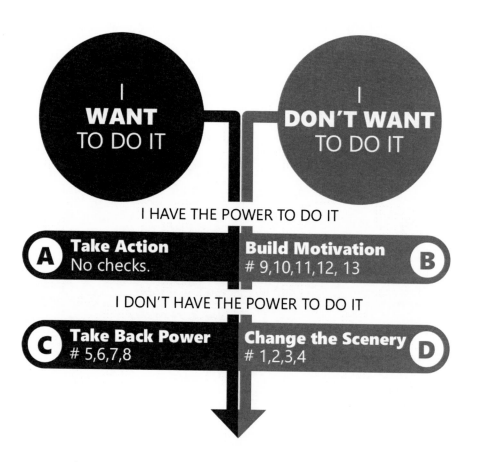

A. Take Action

As athletes chant, "You're ready, you're ready!" You have the motivation and willingness to act in the power you have to make whatever changes are needed to achieve the life you desire. Move on to the next chapter so we can start action planning your next power move.

B. Build Motivation

Sure, you could do it. But do you **want** to do it? Finding the motivation to make a different choice and change your life can be challenging, and yet, it is critical if you are going to live the life you want. One surprising aspect of motivation is that it often follows action.[12] You do not "get motivated" and then start an aggressive workout program. Instead, you start working out (many times grudgingly), and through the process, find the motivation to continue. It is the same way when looking for a job, changing your career, or building new relationships. If you need motivation, start small. Start by writing down things you *could* do if you had the motivation. Then identify the smallest step that would require the least amount of work to test and grow your motivation over time. It could be making one call, sending one email, doing one google search, or writing down your thoughts. Afterwards, keep finding one more thing to do until your motivation for the bigger actions have grown, or until you realize that this path is not the one you want to pursue.

C. Take Back Your Power

Giving away our power can happen slowly and easily. It often begins with our language. We get in a habit of using victim-type language. Instead of saying we "get to go to work," we say we "have to go to work." We indicate that other people "bring out the worst in us" as though we have no control over our thoughts and actions. We say that other people's moods "bring us down"

50

or we think "I had to say yes" when in reality a no would have done just fine. To take back your power, start with your language. Invite a friend to help you. Choose someone to whom you often complain. Tell them you are not going to complain anymore and give them the authority to stop you when you do. We cannot say "we're stuck" and at the same time believe we can make a change. They don't go together. Our language has to change followed by our belief that we have the power needed to create the life we desire.

D. Change the Scenery

Sometimes we do not have the motivation *or* the belief that we can do something different. I struggled with my weight for decades, and still do from time to time. There were many times when I felt powerless and had no energy or interest in making a change. If you are in that place, change your scenery. It is hard to be motivated to do something different when you are surrounded by other non-motivated and non-active people. Instead, you have to put yourself around people, places, and information that are aligned with where you want to be – even if that is light years away from where you are now. If you are lacking the motivation and belief that you can do something different, change your scenery. Find webinars, books, groups, or people that encourage you. Keep putting yourself in those places until you build either the motivation or the belief that what you want can and should be done.

The Good News

Many of us end up in certain jobs or careers because our parents said "that would be a good job." What did we know? We knew absolutely nothing, so we did it. Regardless of how you ended up where you are, it is your responsibility to change it if you want to. If you are unhappy, I hope that you want a change. It does not matter if someone else was the cause of you being where you are. It is still your responsibility to change it if it is not where you want to be.

You may have heard that the good news of knowing you are the problem, is that you now know that *you* are also the solution. Challenges, problems, and obstacles will continue to get in your way. In fact, I can promise you there is no clear path to success. Every person will face obstacles– there may be challenges in our upbringing that influence our mindset, bad habits that get in our way, or difficult circumstances like the unexpected loss of someone you love. In all of those circumstances, the answer for how you will get from where you are to where you want to be is still *you*. To begin that process, start with believing you have the power and can build the motivation to make the changes needed. I would rather us die on the road to our best life than live every day having never taken a step. Wouldn't you?

Chapter Summary:
- Power is not a dirty word.

- Assessing your current sense of power and motivation can help you identify what to do next.
- You have the power you need to change your life.

Take Action:

1. Congratulations – you have been promoted! Pretend you are the president of your country or the CEO of your organization. What are three things you would do for YOU to help you achieve your career goals? Now do them for yourself as much as you can.

2. Avoid victim language for the next three days. Change "have to" to "get to." Stop all complaining about your manager, spouse, partner, friends, and co-workers. You have chosen to work with them and be in those relationships. Notice how much power you gain from assuming the power you have already been given.

3. Change your scenery. Visit a local place you've never been before that is related to something of interest. Invite someone new to lunch. Attend a lecture. Do something out of the ordinary to expose yourself to new people, places, and ides.

6

Create Options

"Life is about choices."

– Julia L. Pace, Secondary Educator

"It's a mistake to try to look too far ahead.
The chain of destiny can only be grasped one link
at a time."

-   Sir Winston Churchill

There is a purpose and journey for *your* life. You can learn from others, but 'others' do not have your history, your upbringing, or your gifts. Your journey will be different from theirs. I learn from other people every day but, at the end of the day, I have to make the decisions over my life, and I respect other people's right to do the same. Several people have asked me 'how did you have the courage to leave your steady job and salary?" My answer is that it was (and is) a combination of Faith, Investing the Right Energy in the Decision, Betting on Myself, and Taking Action. Through these steps, you can create a series of Action Options. These options will become the beginning of your Action Plan. As you read this chapter, use the worksheet to write down any actions that come to mind. We are going to need those later as you begin to act.

Have Faith

You will not know the end from the beginning so you can stop looking for it. My second year as a presenter at TD Jakes' Megafest (a faith-based lifestyle conference), I led a session on defining and obtaining career success. There were hundreds of people in the room that shared that they felt 'stuck'. They were working in something they did not want to do and had not taken steps to move forward into their dream career or business. I asked the group how many people knew one next step that they should take and over 80% of the people raised their hands. That was mind boggling to me. Eighty percent of the people knew something they could do to move forward but were frozen, unable to take that step. Why? The most common reason cited was they did not know how it was going to work out in the end. They could see the beginning, but they had no idea how they were going to get to the end. Can I tell you something? This may be disappointing, or it may be liberating. You are never going to know the end from the beginning. You can think about it, journal about it, go to conferences, pray on it, and everything else. However, the end is rarely revealed from the beginning – at least not in the level of detail most of us want to be comfortable to act.

Moving into your dreams is going to require faith. For me, it was faith that my Creator, who loves me with a depth I will never understand, would be with me through the next steps in my life.

Faith that He did not give me a dream to then torture me with the inability to achieve it. Faith that when I make mistakes (and I did and do), He will help me through and I will be better for it. During a school visit with my daughter, a high school counselor shared with her that faith is living life forward, even though you may only understand it backwards.

If you are waiting to know the end, and how it will work out, you will be waiting forever. One hundred percent certainty in life is rare and unrealistic. There is uncertainty and risk in every life and career decision that we make. Your certainty may be particularly low at the beginning, so guard against expecting anything more. **Instead, take the next step.** Only then will the next step or next phase of the plan be revealed. The business I have now is quite different than the business I imagined I was going to have when I launched, and so is my life. I never envisioned writing a book, delivering leadership training in ministry, creating and co-hosting a radio show and podcast, creating an email group to spur people on in their careers and life, or hiring family and friends to work alongside me in the business. I never imagined any of it, but that is exactly the life I am living.

Invest the Right Energy

Making good decisions about your career and life requires a high degree of mental energy.[1] Research suggests that with fatigue, illness, or distraction, our decision quality suffers.[2] Imagine coming home late after working several 12-hour days and then deciding what you're going to eat for dinner. Cereal anyone? To make quality decisions, we need to be full of energy, physically well (or as well as feasible for the moment), and focused.

Choose the Time

When do you have your best energy? My best energy is mid-morning. While writing this book, I typically started writing in the first half of the day when I had the greatest physical and mental energy, and when I felt at my best. I have worked with people in different parts of the world and had to join conference calls as early as 5:00 am or as late as 9:00 pm. While I may be present at those times, I am not at my best. What are the times when you are at your best? Choose those windows for getting your most important work and thinking done.

Conserve Energy Where You Can

Conserve your precious mental energy whenever possible.[3,4] You can do this by making low-risk decisions quickly or efficiently. For example, if you are deciding where to go to lunch today, feel free to make a quick decision. Research suggests we make over 200 decisions about food each day.[5] You can afford to gamble on a lunch decision. Go with your first thought and do not spend energy rethinking the decision. That is deciding quickly.

The other option is to make low-risk decisions efficiently. Meaning, make it once so you don't have to make it again. When

I consulted with GE, they gave me a template to use for all presentations. The logo was in the corner, it used black font of a certain type and size, and you were not allowed to add pictures. That saved me an enormous amount of time and energy. I am a creative person, and I love dabbling in graphic design. To me, creating a presentation can feel like an artistic endeavor (in other words, it can take me a ridiculous amount of time). Is that really where I want to spend my precious mental energy? For most areas, probably not. For low-risk decisions, you can make them once and use that same decision repeatedly. Efficiency is why my stats professor Dr. Coates wore the same khaki pants and blue button down every-day, it is why I eat the same breakfast almost every day (yogurt with fruit and nuts + coffee), and it is why President Barack Obama famously responded to low-priority emails with "Agree, Disagree, or Discuss." Make the low-risk decisions once and save your mental energy for decisions that matter.[3]

Invest Your Energy in Big Decisions

Decisions about your career, where to live, who to partner with, how to prioritize your time, and what to study in school have major impacts on your life. Those decisions should not be made quickly or efficiently. Instead, these decisions should be made thoroughly. Create a set of filters that help you make the big decisions of life. For big decisions, I do the following: Write, Meditate, Consult, Settle, and Decide.

Write

If I am starting to feel like I should make a large shift in my life, my first step is to write down my thoughts. It helps me gain clarity on what is already in my mind. It also creates a certain amount of distance from it, so I can walk away from it and come back to it later to review and consider. I can be impulsive, and my first idea may not be my best. So I need time to write it down and reflect on it before moving forward. As Barbara Markway has stated, "there's simply no better way to learn about your thought processes than to write them down."[6] Along with reducing stress and anxiety, journaling is known to help with calming and clearing your mind, letting go of negative thoughts, and increasing your self-awareness.[7] If you are considering taking action, and especially big actions, start by writing them down.

Meditate

While this happens throughout the process, I also spend dedicated time in meditation. For me, I am asking God for wisdom and guidance on the decision. If I don't hear an answer, I will do things that take me deeper into meditation – like fasting from certain foods, turning off the radio in the car so I can experience more silence, and going on silent walks. I will stay here until I feel confirmed to move forward or not. I considered leaving my job five years before I left. I was applying for different professor positions that always fell through at the last minute. While I may want a certain thing, if it is not the right time, it's not worth my energy in pursuing; at least not at the moment. Every time I have chosen purpose over ambition, it has worked in my favor in the end. So give yourself the gift of meditation to go deeper, and give yourself time to consider your decision.

Consult

If I feel confirmation to go forward, I consult with others who can help me get there. I am generally not asking them *if* I should go forward. Instead, I'm gathering their insights, support, and ideas, on *how* to go forward. The right people can also provide support for the journey ahead. Do you have "your people?" Do you have people in your life who motivate and critique? People that encourage, challenge, and fuel your dreams? If you don't have them, go find them. Supportive people can provide a level of encouragement, insight, optimism and energy that propels your journey forward.[8] There are tons of examples of individuals who have made bold decisions on their own, and there are certainly times when you have to go against the crowd. However, making change is easier with a supportive group who can understand and support your way forward.

Settle & Decide

I allow my mind to settle on the right actions. There are often lots of things I *could* do in service to the change I am making. I want to feel confirmed that I am starting with the right next step, and this can take a while. Other people may pressure you into making a decision on their timetable. Resist it. Only you can decide when it is time to take action and move. I felt strongly led to leave my last job 9 months before I actually turned in my notice. I knew I was going to do it, but those 9 months were needed to orchestrate the how, the timing, and the support needed to make it a success. Take the time needed to settle and confirm your thinking so you can move forward with confidence. Just don't take forever. If you are someone who tends to procrastinate, you may want to set an ideal timeline to give yourself something to work towards.

Bet on Yourself

Some people tried to talk me out of leaving my job and launching my business. At the root, they were scared for me. I had achieved a level of security and stability, and they did not want me to walk away from it and regret it later. I completely understood and appreciated their perspective and concern. In fact, research demonstrates that those around us that resist or disagree with our direction can provide an important counter-balance to ensure we are making informed and realistic decisions.[9,10,11] However, I remember telling someone, "I understand your concern, but sometimes you have to bet on yourself." And I meant it. I had worked for over 20 years in various corporate jobs and had generally (except for one manager – I will save that story for another time), received excellent performance reviews, recognition, and rewards. So after creating the business plan, I remember thinking "If I can do great work for someone else, why can't I do great work for myself?" I made the decision to leave, began my preparations, and nine months later, I turned in my resignation.

One thing that gave me comfort in making a change was my belief that if I am going to make a mistake, it was going to be my own ding dang mistake. I love the counsel of wise advisors. Wise counsel has helped me make great decisions, change my mindset, and avoid mistakes. But after I have received counsel, I make my own decisions. I remember an incident when I was new to an organization. We were trying to resolve a tough issue, and my manager recommended I go to the manager of the person I was working with to get it resolved. I really did not feel comfortable doing it but did it anyway since my manager asked me to. Well of course, the method damaged the relationship with the person I was working with. I ended up calling her to apologize and let her know I would not take that approach in the future. What I learned from that instance, and so many others, is that I have to make my own decisions, which also means making my own mistakes.

Sometimes I cannot explain my decisions to others, but that's okay because, for most people, their agreement is not required for me to move forward. What is required, is for me to make the decision that I know I should make. Then, when I make a mistake, I can fully own up to it and get it resolved; and avoid the greater regret of a decision that I knew was wrong from the beginning. The only human in my life that has veto power on the decisions I make is my husband. As life-partners, our decisions need to be aligned. I remember when we were considering foster care and adoption, a counselor told us it takes two yeses and one no to make the decision. And that is generally how we have lived our life. Major changes require both of our agreement, which is also why your choice of who you will spend your life with is so incredibly important.

Take Action

This is either the exciting part, the scary part, or both. When asked how they felt when making a career move, one that had a significant impact on their life, people often described experiencing two emotions: excitement and fear. Regardless of your feelings at this point, it is time to act. Begin moving. Take a step.

If you are going to live the life you were created to live, many decisions and actions are required. I love the origin of the word decision. "De" means off, "Cis" is to cut, and "Sion" is the state of. So *decisions* are the state of cutting off. What are you cutting off? Options. One challenge of today's information-rich society is that we have so many options. The coffee aisle of my local grocery store has over 50 options. Those options can create a state of paralysis as we consider and peruse each one. Sometimes we do what I call *Procrasti-planning*. We disguise our unwillingness to decide with planning. However, planning is not doing. It's not bad, but it is not action, and we cannot confuse the two.

To live YOUR life, get ready to make decisions. A lot of them. And get ready to take action. Lots of it. The more you decide and act, the more comfortable you will become. Research suggests that when we make decisions that are in alignment with our values and core beliefs, we feel more positive, and that positivity can encourage us to do more of the same. Do you need to get more comfortable making decisions? Try the action steps below. Also, commit to doing the thing that is next on your list within the next seven days. Yes, that may require reworking your schedule and plan. Get used to it. That will be required as well.

Chapter Summary:

- You may not know the end from the beginning. Stop expecting it.
- We should expect to make lots of decisions and take lots of action.
- To identify and take the actions needed, get ready to demonstrate faith, invest the right energy, bet on yourself, and act.

Take Action:

1. **Make Small Decisions Quickly.** In my personal life, I was in the habit of abdicating my decisions. I am not sure if I thought I was being nice, or if it was led by

my insane need to please. Let me give you a few examples to see if they sound familiar to you.

Hubby: Where do you want to go to dinner?
Me: I don't know, you can choose.

Friend: What movie do you want to see?
Me: Hmmm...What do you want to see?"

If both parties are decision-abdicators, you are really in trouble. Where do you want to go? I don't know, where do you want to go? Ugh! Come on people. Get comfortable speaking your mind. Sharing your perspective does not mean the other person has to agree with you, but it does give them an opportunity to consider a different perspective. Next time someone asks you a question, instead of abdicating your decision, give yourself a moment and answer truthfully.

Hubby: Where do you want to go to dinner?
Me: Pappadeaux's. Where would you like to go?

Isn't that a lot simpler? To make good decisions and identify the right action steps, we have to be good at making decisions and hearing from others. For the next seven days, try sharing your perspective, honestly.

You may find that it takes you a while to provide it because you're not used to considering or voicing your own feelings on a matter.

If you make decisions and share your perspective effortlessly, consider how you can encourage this behavior in those around you. If you are a quick decision maker, others may simply opt out of sharing their perspective when they are in your presence. They find it easier to go with your plan than to invest the time, energy, and sometimes courage, it requires to share their own. If you are not hearing from others, you are missing out on ideas, insights, and perspectives that may take your endeavors to the next level.

2. Write down any next steps that are in your mind at this moment. It does not matter if you think they are the 'right' next steps. Just get those thoughts and actions out of your head and onto paper. We can evaluate them later. Come back to this list any time you get a new action idea. Keep a running list of actions to consider.

7

Make Change

"Did you get your lesson out?"
– Johnny L. Pace, Ret. Lt. Col, US Army

The strategies I use to manage life today are very different from the strategies I used five years ago. I expect the same level of change five years from now. Moving to new places requires new knowledge, skills, and ways of thinking. Not up for it? Sound exhausting? It is not. What *is* exhausting is going to a job you do not enjoy, living with mediocre relationships, and wishing for things you will never have. When you are working in your purpose, there is peace and fulfillment. I regularly work on Friday afternoons, Saturday mornings, and week-day evenings. I go to weeknight association meetings to learn, share and connect, and very little of it is exhausting.

To live the life you desire is going to require change from the inside out. Three areas you may have to change, and examples of changes I have made include: adapting your mindset, increasing your skillset, and expanding your peopleset. Let's get started.

Adapting Mindset

Wisdom can be found anywhere though it is certainly not found everywhere. Some of my greatest life lessons have come from distinctly different places such as soap operas (thank you General Hospital!) and the Bible. Often times I will hear something and it will lead me to search for the truth of that wisdom in my faith. To live a different life than you have today, learning must be your constant companion.

One of the greatest lessons I have learned since starting a business is that sometimes we are healed 'as we go'. In your own business, there is little time for sick days. I had experienced migraines since the age of seven. They would regularly keep me in the bed for a day (or two), avoiding light, not able to keep one thing in my stomach, missing events, and not able to interact with my family. When I started my own business, and it was just me, I quickly realized there was no one available to back me up when I had a migraine and couldn't make it. Yes, I was sick, but I had to learn to do it anyway. Sometimes that "it" was leading a training session with enthusiasm, sometimes that "it" was meeting with clients, and sometimes that "it" was taking care of back-end business items. Whatever it was, I had to do it. My previous mindset of "the body needs rest" and "if I am sick I need to go home and rest" had to go.

Instead, I adopted a mindset that I will be healed as I go; meaning, I was going to do what I had to do, and the healing would come along. Three years into the business, I was still struggling with migraines. I was going and doing, but the healing was not coming. I was still executing all of the business activities, but I was sick as a dog while doing some of them. Working while sick eventually got me to a place of deciding that migraines had to go. Period. The end. After this decision, I went deep in learning about migraines, the body, healing, and how others had escaped this lifelong torture. I read, watched a gazillion YouTube sermons on the topic (okay, not a gazillion, but definitely a lot), spoke to my mentors about it and they prayed over me, talked to my husband and he would lay hands on me and pray for me whenever I wasn't well, and several other things. About a year after this decision, and investing the time in believing learning, and changing my mindset, the migraines were virtually gone. I had found a new way of eating and living that began a health transformation, relieved me of migraines, and also relieved me of the guilt of overeating. The guilt release may have been just as much of a relief as the migraines going away.

In all of that, the thing that changed first was my mindset. I had to decide that sickness was not going to control me – I was going to do what I had to do even if I had to do it sick. I had to believe that healing from migraines was possible and spend time learning about how it happened for others. I had to listen to a dear friend of mine who suggested a different way of eating as a method of relief having no idea that it was going to lead to me being healed from a condition I had struggled with for forty years.

I am certainly not saying that all of life's circumstances will change because of our mindset. However, we do have the opportunity to change our perspective even if the circumstances stay the same. Even if my migraines had never gone away, the change in my mindset allowed me to approach my work with a different perspective than I had in the past. In what area do you need to adjust your mindset to get what you want most? What beliefs are getting in your way and have to go? Adapting your mindset and way of thinking is the first step toward real and lasting change.

Increasing Skillset

Not being good at something does not mean you are not called to do it. I used to believe that if I was supposed to do something, I would pick it up easily. However, life has taught me that is just not true. In a landmark study, Dr. Benjamin Bloom, a professor at the University of Chicago, studied 120 elite adult performers. Other than the impact of height and size for athletes, he found that expertise in adults could be explained by their intense practice, committed teachers, and family support. Dr Bloom's summary was that *"Consistently and overwhelmingly, the evidence showed that experts are always made, not born."* [1] This research was then replicated across many domains including medicine, acting, chess, writing, programming, dance, music, aviation, and firefighting among others. In summary, this means that you have the ability to gain almost any skillset that you desire if you are willing to work hard enough, for a long enough time.

Personally, I love art. Paintings, tapestry, graffiti art, artistry in dance and music, all of it. For most of my life I admired artists, but never considered *becoming* an artist because I was not good at it. I thought great artists were child virtuosos. I assumed they had each painted beautiful masterpieces from the time they picked up the brush. How wrong I was. Becoming an artist, like anything else, is developed with practice, over time. While your genetic and biological gifting may help, your work ethic and willingness to practice is what turns an amateur (this is fun!) into a professional (this is fun *and* I get paid!). Even Wolfgang Amadeus Mozart, who may be the most famous child prodigy, had a background that pointed to the influence of practice and mentoring. Mozart's father was a skilled musician, composer, and teacher who put aside his own work to invest in teaching and publicizing the work of his son at a young age. Prince, a modern-day musical genius, was reported to record a piece of music almost every day. Let that sink in – a new piece of music every day. Some may say his talent drove his recordings; however, it is also true that his recordings built his talent. Chihuly, the pioneering glass artist, began school in a different artistic area several years before creating his first blown glass artwork for which he would later become famous. I love the Michael Jordan commercial where he says, "Maybe I led you to believe it was easy when it wasn't...Maybe I led you to believe that basketball was a God-given gift, and not something I worked for...every single day of my life." If you assumed like I did that not being *naturally* good at something is a sign that it is not for you, then change your mindset and get ready to work.

Many of us have told ourselves that we are not good at something for years and have nurtured the belief that it is based on our innate abilities. How many times have you used the phrase, "I am just not good at _____." I have said things like "I'm just not good with names" as an excuse to forget other people's names. I've said "I'm not good with details" as an excuse to only focus on the portions of work I enjoy. More accurate statements would be "I don't enjoy working with details" and "I need to focus more on learning each person's name." Both of those statements still accurately depict that I'm not good at it but attribute this lack of skill to the right areas – lack of interest and lack of focus. Research has demonstrated that trainees who attribute their lack of performance to stable, innate abilities lose motivation, satisfaction, and the belief that their performance can improve.[2,3] In other words, when we tell ourselves we *can't* do something, we lose motivation and stop believing it will ever happen. On the flipside, trainees that believed their lack of performance was due to factors they could control, put forth greater effort and adapted their learning strategies to gain the skills they need to succeed.[3]

Interestingly, the opposite way of thinking – believing that your strengths are natural - can be just as detrimental as believing that your weaknesses are natural. Many of us assume that our strengths are the result of our natural gifts instead of practice, work, or experience. I was really good at school from an early age and remember believing that I was great at taking tests, and I was. If someone had asked me why, I would have told them 'I don't know. It has always come easy to me.' One day, when preparing for a training class delivery, I challenged myself to think about why I was good at test taking. Was it because of natural talent? Possibly, but there were other options to consider. Perhaps it was because I went to private school for two years before moving to a public school that was one year behind my private school. When I arrived at the public school, I was considered "gifted" but mainly because I was one year ahead in learning. Also, my mom was an English teacher, and my dad was a military officer who was insistent on us studying (or "getting our lesson out" to use his term). I also had three older sisters who led the way in school and homework. And in middle school, I took a summer course at a community college on studying and test-taking and used most of those strategies throughout my education. So, was I good at test-taking naturally, or did I have experiences that increased my ability to take tests? Maybe both, but I cannot negate the impact of the skill-building experiences and positive mentors in my life.

Think about your strengths. Were they given to you at birth? Have you had experiences and teachers that helped to turn those traits into the strengths that you demonstrate today? My guess is that your experiences explain some if not most of the strengths you exhibit today. The danger of believing your strengths are naturally given is that you will not invest in them to grow them, and keep them sharp and up to date. Nothing on Earth stays the same. Your strengths are either growing or falling behind. Research indicates that consistently practicing and investing in your strengths is what keeps you at the top of your game. Musicians over 60 years old, who have continued to practice for several hours a week, can match the speed and technical skills of 20-year-old expert musicians. In a study of physicians, researchers found that the longer physicians have been out of training, the less able they are to identify unusual diseases of the lungs or heart. Performance returned only after the doctors underwent a refresher course.[4] So not only do we need to build a skillset, we need to continue investing in that skillset to maintain and grow it over time.

Have you fallen into the trap of believing that if you are not good at something, you were not meant to do it? Or conversely, that you are good at things because they are natural gifts only? That thinking will keep you from investing the time needed to develop and grow the skillset you need to live the life you want. As a result of this revelation, I now look at a missing skillset as something I have yet to build. My daughter and I watch reality

74

television, and I can tell you that some people are terrible at relationships – or at least they appear that way on TV. They may be too giving, too selfish, mean-spirited, self-absorbed, too shy, arrogant, or any other number of habits that get in the way of meaningful relationships. Does this mean they will never have the type of relationship they want? Of course not! We can build relationships skills just like we can build artistic skills, technical skills, and manager skills.

When I started my business, I had never taken an entrepreneurial class or run a business. I was always in the middle of the pack in Girl Scout cookie sales and all other sales initiatives I participated in as a child and adult. I was not known as a 'sales' person and thought sales would be my biggest hurdle to overcome in owning a business. I mean, who was going to sell what I offered? I quickly learned that I would be the seller of my offerings. I also learned that I was going to be the administrative assistant, marketer, website designer, finance manager, project manager, and every other role there was until I could make enough money to hire other, more competent people to do it. To make things work when starting out, I was and continue to be, in a constant mode of improving my skillsets. I have gotten better at introducing myself and my business, have become semi-knowledgeable about website design, and have learned that I have an eye for marketing graphics and design; all of which are skillsets I have built since starting the business. I also recently started investing time in producing, and not just admiring different mediums of art, and I am loving it.

What if you are like me and you don't have the skillsets you need to live the life you want? Not a problem! You can learn it. Almost anything can be learned from the internet, books, classes, or mentors who are willing to teach you what they know. I learned from a book how to start my day to ensure each day is wildly productive. I pulled together information from books and mentors to create a method for managing and closing sales calls. And I found amazing and talented people to teach me how to do what I could not....or not yet anyway. You can build the skillsets you need too.

A Quick Note: YouTube is not Enough. Learning new skills is not about a new degree, though that could certainly be part of the answer. A new skillset is far more than education, watching videos, or reading books. I can watch videos all day about sailing – that does not mean I am ready to navigate a sailboat. Research has demonstrated that most of us over-estimate our ability to do something based on observation alone. I call it the YouTube Effect. That is why so many of us watch someone do something on YouTube and say "I could do that" and believe it is something we could accomplish the next day. We tell ourselves 'I could sell t-shirts', 'I could start a make-up company'. Yes, you absolutely could. However, we cannot be naïve to think that we can do it without the preparation, learning, and actual practice required to build our skills. When building your skills, be sure to go beyond videos by adding *doing* options that allow you to practice and improve.

Expanding Peopleset

Your people are out there, and it is your responsibility to find them. What do I mean by "your people?" So many things! In the last several decades, Western society has become more and more isolated. If we are not alone, we are isolated in our nuclear families. Many of us do not know what living in a community is like. Instead, we have over-invested in self-reliance, and are living isolated, and often lonely lives. The percentage of adults who report being lonely has increased from 20% in the 1980s to 40% in 2019.[5] We have moved to the suburbs for more space, moved towns for our careers, increased our obsession with individual success, and spent most of our 'down-time' alone...on our phones. This level of isolation has an impact. We know that people often find their purpose in connection with the right others. How can you form deep connections with others in today's environment? It is tough. Let's explore how you can find your others - *your people* who can support, encourage, and spur you along to your purpose; and for whom, you can do the same in return.

It Takes Time. Your Time.

When we moved to Texas, we joined a church that was being started by friends of ours. One of the missions of the church was to create a community. I recall my pastor preaching many sermons that described how community was formed and all of those things required more of our time. He explained that you cannot run out of the church right after service is over, waving at everyone and talking to no one, and expect to build a community. You also can't decline every invitation for a friendship or 'non-essential' gathering and expect to live in community; but that is exactly what I did for several years of my life. Research shows that many working adults de-prioritize friendships when considering their long list of other work and life demands.[6,7] As a result, finding people you can connect with outside of work and family will take intentional effort and time. Research also suggests this effort is worth it. Friends are more likely than your family to be empathetic and provide more genuine support and encouragement.[8,9] Why? There are complex histories and dynamics within the family structure that are absent in many adult friendships. Adult friendships are known to increase self-esteem which in turn, is related to more positive life outcomes. So if you are like I was, and have chosen not to fully invest in friendships, it is time to make room on your calendar for a different choice.

My husband's grandmother, Pearl C. Green, often said "show me who your friends are and I'll show you who you are." If you look around at your friends right now, who are you? Are you the person you most want to be? Do your friends encourage and inspire you? Do they motivate you to do better and live a more abundant life? If not, it is time to expand your circle. You can think about the quality of your friendships as it relates to your purpose in three categories – What, How, and Why.

What

Do you have friends that are doing *what you want to do*? If not, find some. I met with several business owners when I started my business. Most were extremely generous and kind with their knowledge, contacts, and insights. Some were just terrible, but the good far outweighed the bad. Consider who is already in your network and start there. If you do not have people you know, begin by putting yourself where those other people might be -- attend industry or topical groups and meet-ups, join social media groups for like-minded people in your area, take a webinar or class from someone who is doing amazing things in your space. Learning from talented others is an essential part of your growth and development. If you are not spending time with others who are talented in your area, that is the first place to start.

"For by wise guidance you will wage war,
And in abundance of counselors there is victory"
     - *King Solomon, Proverbs 24:6*

How

Do you have friends that operate in a way that aligns with how you want to show up? My people are amazing. I have friends who tell it straight and keep me from being too much of a cream puff. I have friends who are ultra-health conscious and inspire me to live a healthier life. I have friends who are deeply involved in the community that inspire me to give and do more. I have friends that are Bible-scholars with whom I can discuss and debate various topics. I also have friends who are super negative, complain a lot, avoid spiritual topics, and don't walk in their power. I'm not saying that every person you interact with needs to inspire you to be more, but I am saying that you need a healthy number of such friends. If you have stopped picking up the phone when your friends call because you are done with that energy, it is time to expand your circle. I am personally not a fan of ending friendships that do not inspire me because who knows, maybe I am there to inspire them. And plus, none of us show up at our best in every moment. What I do need is a healthy balance of people who are inspiring me to be greater and live in alignment with my purpose.

Why

Lastly, do you have friends who need what you provide? In other words, who are you serving? The gifts you have can benefit someone else. In order to discover and live inside your purpose, you have to know who you are called to serve. These people may be in your family, your neighborhood, or across the world. One way we can confirm our calling is through action. By serving in certain areas, you learn what you are, and are not called to do. If you are not already doing it, begin by serving the people you are called to help. If you are planning to start an IT business for small business owners, begin by identifying and serving small business owners in your circle. Ask about their needs and find out how you can best solve their challenges and grow their business. Do you feel called to healthcare? Become a candy striper (yes, they still exist). Get busy serving someone that is connected to your purpose. Through service, you will either be confirmed in moving forward or confirmed in going another direction. Either is helpful on the journey.

Chapter Summary:

- Living the life you desire is going to require change from the inside out.
- Three areas you may have to change are your Mindset, Skillset, and Peopleset.

Take Action:

1. When you read the chapter, what changes did you identify that may be necessary?
2. Do you need to adapt your mindset? Increase your skillset? Expand your peopleset?
3. Write down the ideas under the Action Options section of the worksheet. No need to take action now. That is coming soon enough.

Part 2 Summary

Look Out: Create Options

You have finished Part 2! At this time, you should have a list of action options that you could possibly take. It does not mean you are going to complete all of those actions, but you should have a few options captured in the Action Options section of the worksheet. If you do not have any action options listed, now is the time to get creative! Take 30 minutes now and brainstorm some possible actions that can take you from where you are to where you want to be.

"The most creative act you will ever take is the act of creating yourself."

– Deepak Chopra

8

Set Goals: One Month & Three Years

"Look closely at the present you are constructing:
it should look like the future you are dreaming."
— Alice Walker

I am very goal focused. *Very.* When I worked in corporate roles, I kept my objectives for the year printed and referred to them often. In my business, I started with a vision statement and financial goals. During my first year in business, I met numerous business owners who had been in business for years without making a profit. I realize there are some businesses that are asset and intellectually heavy on the front-end and require a significant investment to succeed - Walt Disney, Twitter, and WordPress to name a few. But for me and the goals I had at the time, that was not going to work.

When I launched my first business, I was focused on helping others achieve their goals and I was clear that I also wanted to achieve mine. I had walked away from a salary, bonus, and stock options and wanted those replaced as soon as possible. So every day, I prioritized money-generating activities. I am not saying those were the activities I preferred. No, what I preferred was playing with my website, researching new techniques, meeting with friends to talk about business, editing PowerPoints, coaching my friends, and cleaning my office. Those were all 'business-related' activities, but unfortunately, they were not revenue generating. So they happened a lot less than the others. Not because I liked them less or they were generally less important, but because they were significantly less important in meeting the goals I had identified.

During my first week in business, a friend of mine connected me to one of her clients as a potential resource for some work they needed done. I focused all of my best energy on preparing for this meeting as it was the most likely revenue-generating activity on my list. I also spent time following up with contacts, responding to congratulatory notes, and working as a sub-contractor with larger vendors – all in an effort to contribute dollars to the account, and ultimately our family. And with God's blessing, I was profitable in the first month of being in business.

While I was profitable in month one, it took me three years to fully replace my salary. Three years! Some may think that is fast, but I have friends who replaced their salaries in year one. But when we met with our financial planner, three years after starting the business, and he shared that all of our retirement goals were still on track, I breathed a HUGE sigh of relief. That was also the time I realized that replacing my salary for a business owner was small potatoes. So guess, what? I changed and increased my goals. Changed my focus. I am now investing in two revenue-generating streams: my current business and a new venture with my family. The new business will take a greater investment of time, thinking, and resources before turning a profit; and in my current world, I am okay with that.

Let me tell you what research has proven over and over again: goals work. They work in all aspects of your life. They work even better if you write them down, ensure they are goals you care about, size them for impact, check on them often, and are willing to get honest and get better. Your goals may not be financial. Your goals may be focused on solving certain problems, building certain relationships, or having more fun in life. It does not matter the topic, goal setting still works. To make your goals as helpful and impactful as they can be, implement these five proven strategies:

Write Them Down: Research has proven that people who write down their goals are more likely to achieve them. This has been proven time and time again so I am not going to spend a lot of time on this topic. As the Chinese proverb says, 'the palest ink is better than the most capricious memory.' We have already started, but this is to encourage you to continue. If you have not downloaded the free worksheet, do it now. Grab a pen, journal, or your favorite computer application, and start writing.

Make Your Goals Things You Actually Care About: I have written many goals that I really did not care enough about to achieve. Was it a 'nice to have?' Sure! But 'nice to have' is not enough to motivate me to do the work needed to achieve a new goal in life. Do you really want more kale in your life? If so, awesome! If not, don't write it down and pretend it is going to happen.

Size Them Right - Make them Big and Small: I want you to look at your goals and ask yourself, if I achieved them, would it make a significant difference in my life? Sometimes we set goals so small that even if achieved, it isn't that exciting. For example, running a 5K is more exciting than running around the block. Making one million dollars is more exciting than making a thousand. Research suggests that bigger goals require us to challenge and change in more significant ways than if we are looking to accomplish a smaller goal.[1,2]

With big goals, we all need small steps. Perhaps my big goal is to change careers – that is definitely big enough to require change and make a difference in my life. However, my first step may be talking to someone I know who is working in that area. This will ensure my goals are big in the long-term, and small in the short-term.[1,2] This is the approach you want to take with your goals too.

Check On it Often: My husband is a process engineer. He works in manufacturing and his teams often receive rewards and recognition for achieving big goals. I was working with a client who was looking to do the same, so I asked my husband how he did this; what was it that helped a team to achieve goals that may have seemed insurmountable. His response was "Write it down. Check on it often." Some of us may write it down, but how many of us 'check on it often?'

You have probably noticed that most weight loss programs include a 'check on it often' component. Whether it is food-logging, weigh-ins, or meeting attendance, you are taught to monitor your progress. Research suggests that those who monitor a goal are more likely to achieve it. Checking on your goals provides three additional benefits that are important to achievement. *First*, it ensures we pay attention to the goal we set. It is so easy to get caught up in the moment and set an important goal for your life on Saturday that you have completely forgotten about by Tuesday.[3,4,5] Distractions and life easily get in the way.[6,7] Checking on it often ensures you keep your desired outcome top of mind. *Second*, monitoring your goal reinforces the right behavior.[3,4,5] If I get on a scale and am down 0.2 pounds, it is time to celebrate. Little wins help to encourage the right behaviors that lead to goal attainment. *Thirdly*, monitoring provides the feedback necessary to course correct when needed. What if I get on the scale and I have gained 2 pounds instead of lost them? It then encourages me to go back to some things I may have stopped, or to change some additional aspects of my behavior to achieve the desired outcome.[8,9] Once your goals are written, place them in a visible location that encourages you to check on them often.

Get Honest and Get Better: I once had a colleague who said he did not want to set goals because he would feel bad if he didn't achieve them. In psychology, that is called "The Ostrich Problem."[10] It is essentially being motivated *not* to set or monitor goals, often driven by a desire to maintain a favorable self-image. In other words, I can't fail if I don't try. Some of us know that feeling. It is the feeling you get when someone asks you to try something new. "Hey Arlene, want to play badminton?" And you immediately fear that when you pick up the racquet, the whole world will see and judge you for your lack of athleticism and badminton expertise. Sure, you may be interested in it, but the fear of failing can easily overwhelm the desire to try. There is another way we can view this problem. If you do not achieve your goals or demonstrate the excellence you desire, you do not have to take it as a personal attack on your character. You just do what I tell my daughter to do - enjoy the experience and work harder. I applied to a leadership program in my city and was rejected. I was actually told I was on the waiting list, but you get the point. We all have at least three potential responses to disappointments and poor performance. Below are those three possibilities and how I could have framed and thought about the leadership program that turned me down.

- **One: We can blame the process**. "It wasn't fair. They should have chosen me. They clearly got it wrong."

- **Two: We can rationalize it away** and pretend we didn't want it or need it. "I didn't have time for that program anyway. I can use my time for something else."
- **Three: We can acknowledge what *we* could have done differently** to drive a more positive outcome. "I completed the application last minute, didn't include my most influential references, and somewhat bombed my way through the networking event. I can do better."

All of these could be true. I personally like number one. Honestly, it is probably a combination, and the only one I can control is #3. So I choose to act on #3. I choose to act on the things I can control, and simply try to understand the rest, and so can you. The willingness to self-evaluate your performance with a critical eye is key to goal achievement. Goal achievement is enhanced when we identify our mistakes, understand the root causes, and evaluate how we can approach it differently going forward.

If you are going to accomplish anything exceptional in life (and I know you are!), it's going to require goal setting, work, and an honest look at why key milestones were not achieved. I could not improve the leadership selection process for the program I applied to, but I can always improve myself. This willingness to assess and focus on the development of self is what some call a Learning Orientation.[11,12,13] With a learning orientation, we focus on growing our skills, adapting and mastering new situations, and learning from our experiences – regardless of the outcome of the goal. In research, a learning orientation, which we can all demonstrate, is associated with higher test scores and more positive outcomes. Why? It's the learning, not just the goal attainment, that helps us get better for the next time.

Chapter Summary:

- Goal setting works.
- Goal setting works even better if you write down your goals, ensure they are goals you care about, size them for impact, check on them often, and are willing to honestly evaluate yourself and get better.

Take Action:

1. Identify a goal you had for yourself that you did not achieve. Assess why the goal wasn't achieved and your response to not achieving it. Did you blame the situation, rationalize it away, or identify ways that you could get better?

2. Decide that you are going to achieve your goals. Even if you do not achieve them the first time (or second), believe that they will be achieved. (And I believe it too!).

3. It is time to identify the actions you are actually going to take and set a few goals. Review actions you listed in the Action Options section of the worksheet. Choose one to two that you believe are most important to achieving your desired outcome.

4. Turn your actions into goals by making them specific and time-bound.

5. Write the goals down in the Goal Setting section of the worksheet.

6. Identify at least one thing you can do in the next week in service to your Big Goal. What is one thing that will get you started?

7. Begin taking action THIS WEEK. Once you have completed your first action, write me and let me know by visiting www.arlenepacegreen.com/contact ! I want to encourage you along the way.

Freebie Alert! Need some inspiration? View a snippet of my yearly goals by visiting www.arlenepacegreen.com/bookresources

9

Overcome Fear

"Don't fear your worst-case scenario, plan for it."
– Arlene Pace Green

I remember waking up in the middle of the night about a week after submitting my resignation letter to my job thinking, "What in the world are you doing?! How selfish of you. What if your retirement plans are now thrown off and you and hubby have to work longer? **What in the world are you doing?!** Did you forget you have a child to put through college? What about the bonus you are walking away from? **WHAT IN THE WORLD ARE YOU DOING?!?!"**

And those same thoughts repeated themselves for several more nights during the first three months of my transition from corporate employment to business ownership. During the day, I was taming lions and taking names! At night, it felt like the lions were taming me. What I learned from that experience is that fear is often a companion to change. Several leaders were asked to describe the emotions they felt during their most impactful learning experiences – experiences like taking new jobs, taking on new assignments, and getting promoted to new levels. Do you remember which two emotions were the most common? Excitement. And Fear.

The National Institute of Health estimates that 18-30% of the US adult population experiences anxiety.[2] Psychologists have learned that one of our most common fears is the fear of failure - also called the fear of our ego's death.[1] We've all spent years crafting an image of who we are. Maybe we are the smart one, the funny one, the one who gets it right. We will do, and avoid doing, lots of things to protect that image. But if you are going to live the life you were designed to live (which you are!), occasionally, you have to face your ego and the emotion of fear…and win. Here are some strategies that will help you in this journey.

Through, Not Around

During one of the most difficult periods of my life, the loss of a loved one, I was often sad, distracted, and just generally not well. Fortunately (or unfortunately), I can compartmentalize with the best of them. I doubt most people would have known how unwell I really was. Even at home, I was relatively functional. I remember one day my husband came home and asked, "So how are you doing?" and I am sure he expected me to say, "pretty good." Instead, I broke down into immediate and unstoppable tears. He was shocked. Later that month I was meeting with my Pastor, and he sensed something wasn't right. I'm blessed to have a Pastor who can see right through my compartments (dang it!). In that meeting, I remember him telling me, you have to go THROUGH the pain, not around it. I also remember shaking my head at him through my tears. And every time I would shake my head *no*, he would respond with *yes*.

What I learned over the next couple years was that my Pastor was right. Time does not heal pain and time does not remove fear. Fear is a very patient emotion – you cannot wait it out. Often, the only way to get to the other side of your fear is **through** it. What does *through* mean? To me it meant a few things:

1. **Acknowledging the fear and pain I was experiencing**. There is no use pretending to not be scared when I am. Instead, when I am fearful or in pain, I say how I am feeling out loud. "I am scared." "This is hard." "This hurts." Psychologists have demonstrated that acknowledging and exposing yourself to the fear can actually reduce its negative effects, and I found that to be true for me.

2. **Speak to it**. Next, I would tell the fear, which is essentially an emotion, what we were going to do, and I leaned on my faith to help me through it. So, "I am scared" turned into "I am scared, but God is with me and He is going to get me through this." "This is hard" became "This is hard, but I can do all things through Christ who strengthens me." "This hurts" became "This hurts, but I know You are close to the brokenhearted and you will get me through this." You have to lean on your sources of strength, which for me is my faith, to carry you *through* the fear and *through* the pain.

3. **Acknowledging that AROUND doesn't work.** My attempt to go around the issue was essentially trying to avoid the elephant in the room. The elephant is still there – with all of its size and smell, just waiting to attack you at the most inopportune moments. Yes, I could pretend not to see it, but my path, actions, and demeanor would be different if I pretended it was not there when I knew it was. How do you know when you are avoiding the elephant in your life? For me, it was when I would cry for silly reasons. That generally meant I had accidentally tripped over the elephant in the room I was trying to avoid. So instead of ignoring the elephant, I decided to kick the elephant out of the room -- or at least down the hall. This meant acknowledging it was there and talking with others who helped me identify strategies to deal with it, instead of avoiding it.

Fear is an Emotion, Not a Decision Criteria

For years, I gave fear too much power. If I was scared, I assumed it meant danger ahead. Certainly, there are times that is true. You are driving on icy roads and think about stopping because you are afraid. Good idea! However, many times, it is not a signal of danger at all. A friend of mine shared her acronym for fear which I still use today – False Evidence Appearing Real, and that is honestly what it is most of the time. Fear is an emotion; it is not a decision criterion. You do not have to make decisions based on fear.

In my career, I have delivered a lot of training. It is something people often compliment me on – my ability to explain clearly, help others understand, and create a fun learning environment. But before many of those opportunities, I am incredibly scared. Can't sleep at night scared. Can't eat scared. Hand and voice shaking scared. Wishing I'd never agreed to do it scared. People are always surprised when I share this because apparently it does not show up in my speaking, but it is absolutely there. At times, the fear will leave almost immediately after I start speaking. Other times, it is there to the end.

If I let fear make my decisions, I would have decided a long time ago that training and speaking were not for me. But it is through this same training and speaking that I had some of my most rewarding experiences. I remember delivering a session on "Finding Your Dream Job" at the TD Jakes Megafest Conference to several hundred attendees a few months before I resigned from my corporate role. I loved it – it is still one of the highlights of my career. I loved everything about it. I felt like I was able to give the attendees helpful advice and I stayed for two hours after the event answering individual questions. If I allowed fear to make my decision, I would have declined the engagement and missed out on the opportunity to meet, interact, and share with so many incredible people.

Is fear a real feeling? Yes. Do you have to learn to manage it? Absolutely. Should you let fear decide what you will and will not do? Absolutely not. You have your brain, your faith, and wise advisers for that. Making decisions is not fear's role and you cannot let it take that position in your life. You just can't.

Don't Trade What You Know for What You Don't

I was talking to my husband one day about my business. I had just submitted a proposal for our first six-figure contract and he asked me if I thought we would get it. I told him I thought we would, but I was not sure if I wanted it. He looked at me like I was crazy. He said, "you know that you often go after business you don't want to get?" Ha! He was so right. Why is that? It is because new levels of success bring new levels of the unknown and that can be scary. What if it goes wrong? What if we don't deliver? What if we can't do the work? What if my ego is damaged? When I got the call that we got the contract, I remember feeling excited…and nauseous.

Throughout the next several months of work, our team worked, learned, and had a fantastic time delivering on the project. The clients were happy and so were we. It was the kind of work we love to do. Several times throughout the project, I told myself "Trust the Process." In our work, we often do not know the end from the beginning. We know the process, but not the exact outcome. So instead of focusing on what we did not know, I focused on what we did know, and I do that in other areas of life as well. Chuck Smith, a prominent American pastor, said that when you have a crisis, remember to never trade what you do know for what you don't. Meaning, we will never have all of the answers – especially in new and unfamiliar situations. If you focus so much on what you do *not* know, you will increase the fear factor, and forget to lean and rely on what you *do* know.

With my new business contract, I knew I had a talented team. I knew my team and I knew how to do the work. I knew we had our clients' best interest at heart. What else did I really need? Turns out absolutely nothing. This strategy has also been called Positive Reframing. It is choosing to focus on what you have, rather than what you don't, and it works. Psychologists have found that it is an effective coping strategy for managing anxiety and bouncing back from failure.[3] How can you reframe your current situation to increase your focus on what is right rather than what is missing? How can you focus on what you do know rather than what you do not?

"What If You Burn It All Down?"

When I was considering moving into business ownership, I had several conversations with people I knew that were already doing what I wanted to do. I asked them for advice, guidance, and ideas. I remember sitting in a conference room at work talking to one of my friends and mentors Trey about what I was considering. Trey is super smart, a C-Suite executive, and has a way with candor and words. He had made a similar transition in his career, albeit at a more senior level. He shared that when he made the transition, he and his business partner told themselves that if the whole thing is a bust and we burn the thing down (meaning, we suck), we will just quit and go find jobs doing what we were doing before. Well, 30 years later they are still in business and doing fantastic work. I actually get to partner with him from time to time in my own business. That conversation was so freeing for me. I often said that same thing to myself, "What if you fail?" "What if you burn it all down?" And my answer to that question was the same as his. I will close up shop and go get a job doing what I was doing before. And five years later, I am still in business, doing what I love, with people I love. I am not living for Friday, or dreading Monday. Life is good.

Sometimes the worst-case scenario is not as bad as we think it is. My husband and I are savers, so we definitely ensured we had a cushion in case the business did not start up the way I hoped; and we adjusted our mindset to understand that we would live on his income alone if it took even longer than expected. One strategy for facing and managing your fears, is to realistically imagine the worst-case scenario, and then plan for it. Make it a challenge to overcome instead of an emotion to avoid. Allow your fear to motivate you. What if you burned it all down? What could you do then to manage that scenario?

Some people start passion projects while working a full-time job to build confidence and skill before going full-time into a new career or business. Some people start with taking a class to learn the new skill they want to gain. I am currently pursuing a new business venture and am learning everything I can. My point is, don't fear your worst-case scenario, plan for it. Then, if it happens, you already have your Plan B ready to go. Forty-four percent of small businesses and over fifty percent of start-ups fail within 5 years.[4] So failure in business, career goals, and other areas is definitely possible. Instead of letting it stop you, let it motivate you.

Chapter Summary:

- To live the life you were designed to live, you will have to face your ego and the emotion of fear -- and win.
- There are strategies that will allow you to feel the fear and do it anyway.

Take Action:

1. Write down what you are afraid of. It could be public speaking, swimming, relationships, public failure, financial ruin, anything.
2. Ask yourself what about that fear is making you afraid? Based on the strategies listed, what can you do the next time that fear appears?

3. Identify your worst-case scenario and create a Reasonable Plan B if it were to occur. For example, what if I do not get the new job I am applying for, what will I do next?

10

They Are Waiting On You

"If I didn't define myself for myself, I would be crunched into other people's fantasies for me and eaten alive."

– Audre Lorde

I talked to several people who had made a corporate-to-entrepreneur transition before I took the leap myself. Two of my friends had done *exactly* what I wanted to do. They were invaluable to me in making the transition. Not only did they share their insights, wisdom, work products, and clients, but they showed me it was possible. Had they not gone first, I am not sure I would have had the courage to do it myself. Just like they inspired me, there are others waiting to be inspired by you.

One of my husband's favorite sayings is *do you*. Each of us has to do what we think is best, while releasing ourselves from doing what others want us to do. And by just *doing you*, you will inspire those who need the kind of inspiration you provide. Every other year, my husband takes a camping trip for a couple weeks. He lives in the back-country, does whatever is in the back country (I wouldn't know because I don't go), and enjoys life in the wilderness. Is it something I would do? Nope. But just seeing him fully immerse himself in what he enjoys, has encouraged me to do the same. I recently took a sewing class and loved it. *Him doing him* has encouraged *me to do me* (see our pictures). I have noticed that the more fully I align with what I personally want to do, and how I personally feel called to live my life, the more people I inspire to do the same.

The unexpected benefit of living the life you were intended to live is that it makes you more inspirational and better in other areas of your life too. I am a far better parent than I used to be. I was not bad before, but I was not nearly as present or patient as I am now. I am also a far better wife. Again, I was not terrible before (or at least I hope not), but now I make coffee for Kelvin (some) mornings, actually cook a meal a few nights a week which I actually like to do (I thought I hated cooking) and listen when he talks without feeling like I am about to drop from exhaustion. I am also a better friend. Once my mind had time to wander, God gave me the idea of a Women's Bible Study. I hosted two women's bible study series' in my home for friends and my husband and I now lead a life group at our house. Absolutely, without a doubt, none of that would have happened had I not changed to a career that offered me more freedom and time. And I certainly would not be writing this book. As I type, I am sitting on my couch, listening to Chilled Cow on YouTube. Definitely not possible in my previous career.

So, what am I saying? I am telling you that others are waiting on you. *You being you* encourages *them to be them*. It also means that you will be able to show up the way you were designed more often for yourself and others. And that is where your peace is. That is where your joy is. It is time to go get it.

Chapter Summary:
- You being you inspires others to be them.
- Your best self is waiting for you.

Take Action:
1. Get in touch with who you are and what you like to do.
2. Spend time alone. Go on walks, rest quietly on your couch, drive around alone, take a bubble bath, do things that give you quiet time with yourself.
3. Write down any thoughts that come to your mind.

11

A Final Note - Before You Quit Your Job...

"This above all – to thine own self be true"

- Character of Polonius in Hamlet by William Shakespeare

When a friend calls saying they had a bad day and are considering quitting their job, the first thing I recommend is a vacation day instead. Why? Because I want us to be thoughtful and not rash in our decision making. Leaving can feel easy and yet starting something new can be much more difficult.

I have a bit of an impulsive spirit. My first idea is not always my best idea. Before making decisions, I generally give myself a waiting period to confirm that I am making the right decision for now and for later. In that waiting period, I have changed many decisions. You may be just the opposite. Perhaps you overthink decisions and are waiting too long to make decisions you were confirmed to make years ago. My caution in either scenario is to *know thyself* and act accordingly.

Am I for quitting or changing jobs that are not meeting all of your needs? Yes! I did it myself. I just want to ensure that whatever decision you make today, you will be happy that you made it tomorrow as well.

If you are considering quitting your job today, promise me that before doing so, you will read Chapter 6 about creating options and making good decisions. And when you feel confirmed to make a move (and not one second later), DO IT.

Part 3 Summary

Look Forward: Take Action

It is time to act! By now you have identified at least one big goal and one small goal that will move you in the direction you want to go. Now is when the real learning and work begins. Do not delay. Don't put this book aside without actually DOING something that will lead you toward the life you want to live.

"The place in which I'll fit will not exist until I make it." – James Baldwin

Love Your Job Worksheet

Download by going to www.arlenepacegreen.com/bookresources

LOOK IN Building Your Purpose	Write your purpose statement below. SAMPLE: I will serve _____ (who?) by ___ (doing what?) using _____ (what skills?).
LOOK OUT Brainstorming Action Options	Write ideas for actions you can take to move from where you are to where you want to be.
LOOK FORWARD Setting Goals & Timelines	Set your goals below. **Big Goal 1:** _____ To accomplish my Big Goal, I will complete the following smaller goals by _____ (insert date). • • **Big Goal 2:** _____ To accomplish my Big Goal, I will complete the following smaller goals by _____ (insert date): • •

REFERENCES

CHAPTER 2

1. Coleman, J. (2017, October 20). You don't find your purpose, you build it. Harvard Business Review. https://hbr.org/2017/10/you-dont-find-your-purpose-you-build-it.

2. Praskova, A., Creed, P. A., & Hood, M. (2015). Career identity and the complex mediating relationships between career preparatory actions and career progress markers. Journal of Vocational Behavior, 87, 145-153. DOI:https://doi.org/10.1016/j.jvb.2015.01.001

3. Dalla Rosa, A., Vianello, M., & Anselmi, P. (2019). Longitudinal predictors of the development of a calling: New evidence for the a posteriori hypothesis. Journal of Vocational Behavior, 114, 44-56. DOI:https://doi.org/10.1016/j.jvb.2019.02.007

4. Kerpelman, J.L., Pittman, J.F., Lamke, L.K. (1997). Development: An identity control theory approach. Journal of Adolescent Research, 12(3), 325-346.

5. Todd, B. (2016, May). To find work you love, don't (always) follow your passion. 80,000 Hours. https://80000hours.org/articles/dont-follow-your-passion/

6. London, M. (1983). Toward a theory of career motivation. Academy of Management Review, 8, 620-630.

7. Gould, S. (1979). Characteristics of career planners in upwardly mobile occupations. *The Academy of Management Journal, 22*(3), 539-550.

CHAPTER 3

1. Rath, T. & Harter, J. (2010). *Wellbeing: The five essential elements.* Gallup Press.
2. Greenhaus, J. H., & Powell, G. N. (2006). When work and family are allies: A theory of work-family enrichment. *The Academy of Management Review, 31*(1), 72–92.

CHAPTER 4

1. US News & World Report (2020). 100 best jobs https://money.usnews.com/careers/best-jobs/rankings/the-100-best-jobs
2. Barrett, W. P. (2020, December 11). *America's top charities.* Forbes. https://www.forbes.com/lists/top-charities/#43d070705f50
3. Ward, M. (2017). *3 science backed reasons having a hobby will help your career.* CNBC. https://www.cnbc.com/2017/08/02/3-science-backed-reasons-having-a-hobby-will-help-your-career.html
4. Pressman, S. D., Matthews, K. A., Cohen, S., Martire, L. M., Scheier, M., Baum, A., & Schulz, R. (2009).

Association of enjoyable leisure activities with psychological and physical well-being. *Psychosomatic Medicine, 71*(7), 725–732. https://doi.org/10.1097/PSY.0b013e3181ad7978

5. Zawadzki, M. J., Smyth, J.M., Costigan, H. J. (2015). Real time associations between engaging in leisure and daily health and well-being. Annals of Behavioral Medicine, *49* (4), 605–615. https://doi.org/10.1007/s12160-015-9694-3

6. Walker, M (2017, October 24). *Why your brain needs to dream.* Greater Good Magazine. https://greatergood.berkeley.edu/article/item/why_your_brain_needs_to_dream

7. Merriam-Webster (n.d.). Potential. In *Merriam-Webster.com dictionary.* Retrieved December 21, 2020, from https://www.merriam-webster.com

CHAPTER 5

1. Northouse, P. G. (2018). *Leadership: Theory and practice (8th ed.): Chapter 1 Introduction.* Sage Publications.

2. Harter, T (2018, August 26). *Employee engagement on the rise in the US.* Gallup. https://news.gallup.com/poll/241649/employee-engagement-rise.aspx

3. McQuaid, M. (2012, October 16). *Two thirds America unhappy at job.* Business Wire. https://www.businesswire.com/news/home/20121016005 065/en/Two-Thirds-America-Unhappy-Job-65-Choose-Boss

4. Thibaut, J. W., & Kelley, H. H. (1986). *The social psychology of groups.* Transaction Publishers.

5. Luciano, E. C., & Orth, U. (2017). Transitions in romantic relationships and development of self-esteem. *Journal of Personality and Social Psychology, 112*(2), 307-328. DOI:10.1037/pspp0000109

6. Montoya, R. (2008). I'm hot, so I'd say you're not: The influence of objective physical attractiveness on mate selection. *Personality and Social Psychology Bulletin, 34*(10), 1315–1331. DOI:10.1177/0146167208320387

7. Buchko, A. A., Buscher, C., & Buchko, K. J. (2017). Why do good employees stay in bad organizations? *Business Horizons, 60*(5), 729-739. DOI: 10.1016/j.bushor.2017.06.001

8. Bundrant, M. (2011). *Six reasons why people stay in a bad relationship.* iNLP Center. https://inlpcenter.org/bad-relationship/

9. Goleman, D. (1984, March 6). *Excuses: New theory defines their role in life.* New York Times. https://www.nytimes.com/1984/03/06/science/excuses-new-theory-defines-their-role-in-life.html

10. Zetlin, M. (2019, January 26). *Science Shows Why You Should Leave an Unhappy Relationship, Even If You're Scared of Being Single.* Inc. https://www.inc.com/minda-zetlin/unhappy-marriage-partnership-staying-together-splitting-up-children-co-parenting.html

11. Barratt, W. (2012, June 14). *The Barratt Simplified Measure of Social Status (BSMSS).* Social Class on Campus. http://socialclassoncampus.blogspot.com/2012/06/barratt-simplified-measure-of-social.html

12. Clear, J. (2020). *Motivation: The Scientific Guide on How to Get and Stay Motivated.* James Clear. https://jamesclear.com/motivation#What%20is%20Motivation?\

CHAPTER 6

1. Hoomans, J. (2015, March 20). *35,000 Decisions: The Great Choices of Strategic Leaders.* Leading Edge Journal. https://go.roberts.edu/leadingedge/the-great-choices-of-strategic-leaders

2. Collins, B. (2019, March 19). *No you shouldn't make decisions while tired. Here's why.* Forbes. https://www.forbes.com/sites/bryancollinseurope/2019/03/19/no-you-shouldnt-make-decisions-while-tired-heres-why/#289acedf34fa

3. Cohen A. (2015, May 5). *Why you should limit your number of daily decisions.* Entrepreneur. http://entm.ag/1EYeS5O

4. Whitaker, M (2017). *The decision maker: An intentional approach to living the life you want.* Greenleaf Book Group Press.

5. Wansink, B. & Sobal, J. (2007). Mindless eating: The 200 daily food decisions we overlook. *Environment and Behavior, 39,* 106-123. DOI: 10.1177/0013916506295573.

6. Markway, B. (2014, April 13). *How to keep a thought diary to combat anxiety.* Psychology Today. https://www.psychologytoday.com/us/blog/shyness-is-nice/201404/how-keep-thought-diary-combat-anxiety

7. Ackerman, C. E. (2020, December 10). *83 benefits of journaling for depression, anxiety, and stress.* Positive Psychology. https://positivepsychology.com/benefits-of-journaling/

8. Garcia, P. Restubog, S. Bordia, P. Bordia, S, & Roxas, R. (2015). Career optimism: The roles of contextual support and career decision-making self-efficacy. Journal of Vocational Behavior. 88. 10.1016/j.jvb.2015.02.004.

9. Higgins, E. T. (2002). How self-regulation creates distinct values: The case of promotion and prevention decision making. *Journal of Consumer Psychology, 12*(3), 177–191.

10. Ng, E. S. W., Burke, R. J., & Fiksenbaum, L. (2008). Career choice in management: Findings from US MBA students. *Career Development International, 13,* 346-361. https://doi.org/10.1108/13620430810880835

11. Muja, N. & Appelbaum, S. (2012). Cognitive and affective processes underlying career change. *Career Development International, 17*(7), 683-701.DOI: 10.1108/13620431211283814

CHAPTER 7

1. Bloom, B. (1985). *Developing talent in young people.* Ballantine Books.

2. Bandura, A. (1977). Self-efficacy: Toward a unifying theory of behavioral change. *Psychological Review, 84*(2), 191-215.

3. Sitzmann, T., & Ely, K. (2011). A meta-analysis of self-regulated learning in work-related training and educational attainment: What we know and where we need to go. *Psychological Bulletin, 137*(3), 421–442. https://doi.org/10.1037/a0022777

4. Ericsson, K.A., Prietula, M. J., & Cokely, E. T. (2007, July-August). *The making of an expert.* Harvard Business Review. https://hbr.org/2007/07/the-making-of-an-expert

5. Abrams, A. (2019, January 15). *Isolation nation.* Psychology Today. https://www.psychologytoday.com/us/blog/nurturing-self-

compassion/201901/isolation-
nation#:~:text=Sadly%2C%20as%20our%20communities
%20are,and%20disengaged%20than%20ever%20before.
&text=Since%20the%201980s%2C%20the%20percentag
e,20%20percent%20to%2040%20percent.

6. Fingerman, K. L., Hay, E. L., & Birditt, K. S. (2004). The best of ties, the worst of ties: Close, problematic, and ambivalent social relationships. *Journal of Marriage and Family, 66*(3), 792–808.

7. Roberts, S. G. B., & Dunbar, R. I. M. (2011). Communication in social networks: Effects of kinship, network size, and emotional closeness. *Personal Relationships, 18*(3), 439–452.

8. Messeri, P., Silverstein, M., & Litwak, E. (1993). Choosing optimal support groups: A review and reformulation. *Journal of Health and Social Behavior, 34*(2), 122–137. https://doi.org/10.2307/2137239

9. Montpetit, M. A., Nelson, N. A., & Tiberio, S. S. (2017). Daily interactions and affect in older adulthood: Family, friends, and perceived support. *Journal of Happiness Studies: An Interdisciplinary Forum on Subjective Well-Being, 18*(2), 373–388. https://doi.org/10.1007/s10902-016-9730-4

CHAPTER 8

1. Locke, E. A., & Latham, G. P. (1990). *A theory of goal setting & task performance.* Prentice-Hall, Inc.
2. Latham, G. P., & Seijts, G. H. (1999). The effects of proximal and distal goals on performance on a moderately complex task. *Journal of Organizational Behavior, 20*(4), 421–429.
3. Ashford, S. J. (1986). Feedback-seeking in individual adaptation: A resource perspective. *Academy of Management Journal, 29*(3), 465–487.
4. Libera, C. D. & Chelazzi, L. (2006). Visual selective attention and the effects of monetary rewards. *Psychological Science, 17*(3), 222-227. https://doi.org/10.1111/j.1467-9280.2006.01689.x
5. Kluger, A. N., & DeNisi, A. (1998). Feedback interventions: Toward the understanding of a double-edged sword. *Current Directions in Psychological Science, 7*(3), 67–72. https://doi.org/10.1111/1467-8721.ep10772989
6. Wieber, F., Thürmer, J. L., & Gollwitzer, P. M. (2015). Promoting the translation of intentions into action by implementation intentions: Behavioral effects and physiological correlates. *Frontiers in Human Neuroscience, 9,* Article 395. https://doi.org/10.3389/fnhum.2015.00395

7. Hofmann, W., Baumeister, R. F., Förster, G., & Vohs, K. D. (2012). Everyday temptations: An experience sampling study of desire, conflict, and self-control. *Journal of Personality and Social Psychology, 102*(6), 1318–1335. https://doi.org/10.1037/a0026545

8. Carraro, N., & Gaudreau, P. (2013). Spontaneous and experimentally induced action planning and coping planning for physical activity: A meta-analysis. *Psychology of Sport and Exercise, 14*(2), 228–248. https://doi.org/10.1016/j.psychsport.2012.10.004

9. Gollwitzer, P. M., & Sheeran, P. (2006). *Implementation intentions and goal achievement: A meta-analysis of effects and processes.* In M. P. Zanna (Ed.), *Advances in experimental social psychology: Vol. 38. Advances in experimental social psychology, Vol. 38* (p. 69–119). Elsevier Academic Press. https://doi.org/10.1016/S0065-2601(06)38002-1

10. Webb, T. L., Chang, B. P. I., & Benn, Y. (2013). 'The ostrich problem': Motivated avoidance or rejection of information about goal progress. *Social and Personality Psychology Compass, 7(11),* 794–807. https://doi.org/10.1111/spc3.12071

11. Dweck, C. S. (1986). Motivational processes affecting learning. *American Psychologist, 41*(10), 1040–1048. https://doi.org/10.1037/0003-066X.41.10.1040

12. Dweck, C. S., & Leggett, E. L. (1988). A social-cognitive approach to motivation and personality. *Psychological*

Review, 95(2), 256–273. https://doi.org/10.1037/0033-295X.95.2.256

13. Elliott, E. S., & Dweck, C. S. (1988). Goals: An approach to motivation and achievement. *Journal of Personality and Social Psychology, 54*(1), 5-12. https://doi.org/10.1037/0022-3514.54.1.5

CHAPTER 9

1. Karl, A. (2007). *Practical intelligence: The art and science of common sense.* Wiley.

2. National Institute of Health. Retrieved on December 26, 2020. https://www.nimh.nih.gov/health/statistics/any-anxiety-disorder.shtml

3. University of Kent (2011, July 14). *Positive reframing, acceptance and humor are the most effective coping strategies.* ScienceDaily. https://www.sciencedaily.com/releases/2011/07/110704082700.htm

4. Mansfield, M. (2020, June 21). *Startup statistics: The numbers you need to know.* Small Business Trends. https://smallbiztrends.com/2019/03/startup-statistics-small-business.html

Meet the Author

Arlene Pace Green, Ph.D.
- Executive Coach, Leadership Development Speaker, Organizational Psychologist, & Author

Dr. Green's mission is to help you identify and achieve your greatest aspirations. She is the founder of Enelra Talent Solutions, LLC a consulting group that specializes in Executive Coaching and Leadership Development. Arlene is known for her business partnership and ability to collaborate with her clients to bring solutions to complex challenges. Dr. Green has a Ph.D. in Industrial/ Organizational Psychology from Old Dominion University and over 20 years of experience in corporate, consulting, and non-profit environments.

Ask the Author
Arlene would love to connect with you! Visit her online at
www.arlenepacegreen.com.